# BECK

Other titles in the series:

The Clash
Leonard Cohen
Elvis Costello
Tom Waits
Neil Young

# BECK

David Quantick

UNANIMOUS

Published by Unanimous Ltd
12 The Ivories, 6–8 Northampton Street, London N1 2HY



A CIP catalogue record for this book is available from the British Library.

Text editor: Ian Fitzgerald
Project editor: Nicola Birtwisle

ISBN: 0 903318 41 6

Printed in Italy

1 2 3 4 5 6 7 8 9

# CONTENTS

## ACKNOWLEDGEMENTS

I'd like to thank Fred Dellar, the man who knows everything, for his deeply informative help with the facts, and Doug Bear of Rare Records in Australia (www.rarerecords.com.au) for the vinyl. Beck has many excellent fan sites but – for a nice change – the official website, www.beck.com, is one of the best of its kind.

## ONE

# THE STORY

Bek David Campbell was born in Los Angeles. His parents lived in a rooming house near the downtown area. His mom, Bibbe Hansen, had just come from New York and his dad, David Campbell, was from 'up North', meaning Canada. They were very young, his mother being still a teenager when he was born. When he was a child Bek's first name was normalized to 'Beck' by teachers who could not be bothered to spell his name right, and when his parents divorced, he took his mother's maiden name and became Beck Hansen.

One of the staples of the pop star, or film star, or any star, life story is the beginning in dull circumstances which leads to a determination in later life to become interesting, sexy and successful. Famous people are expected to be fired into an exciting future by the sheer mundanity of their childhood, the work-ethic mania of their uncomprehending parents, who always want them to work in a bank or a factory or an undertaker's, or the fact that they lived in some 'horrible' suburb, whose green lawns, blue skies and identical houses would clearly make anyone either go mental with a chainsaw or become a successful recording artiste.

The novelty of Beck Hansen's career is that none of these things happened. He was born into poverty, to young, unusually interesting and exciting parents who may not even have had bank accounts, let alone wanted their son to go into banking, he never went near a suburb and he didn't even get his picture in the high school yearbook (unless there was a category called Most Likely To Have Dropped Out Already Because People Kept Trying To Beat The Crap Out Of Him). Neither trendily blue-collar nor, more typically, white-collar pretending to be blue-collar, Beck Hansen had the kind of early life that would have put most people off anything more complicated than alcoholism. Even after escaping from school, surviving a childhood where he was passed from relative to relative, and living in the poorest circumstances imaginable outside a tramp fetishist's dreams, Beck went on to suffer knock-back after knock-back. The shiny-suited, blond, witty pop star we all love today has, unlike possibly any other musician before him ever, more right than anyone else to be a miserable, bitter failure. Instead, he is a droll, intelligent star, the kind of successful person that mothers can point at and say, 'See? Why can't you be more like Beck?'

None of this seemed particularly likely when Bek Campbell was born in 1970 on the 8th of July at one minute to midnight. He was the first child of extremely young parents, David Campbell and Bibbe Hansen, and was born in a rooming house in Hollywood. Shortly after this, David and Bibbe moved again and lived for a while off Hollywood Boulevard, a street then famous for its slightly tarnished brass plaques engraved with the names of dead film stars. It is a street immortalized in the words of a song released when Beck was about a year old, The Kinks' 'Celluloid Heroes', a street full of the names of people, some 'famous and some you never heard of'. It was also, and still is, well-known for being a place where tourist shops are interspersed with cheap bars, movie theatres and cafés specializing in two-dollar poor people's breakfasts. Impossibly romantic for people who don't live there, Hollywood Boulevard can also be the world's own hellhole for those who do.

If Hollywood Boulevard was an unconventional place to start a life, then Beck's family were equally post-normal. His mother Bibbe was a very Warholian blonde (except that she wasn't actually a man) who, appropriately, used to hang out at Andy Warhol's Factory when very young and even appeared in an (unreleased) movie, *Prison*, with superstar and eponymous subject of a song by British rockers The Cult, Edie Sedgwick.

The Factory was a loose collection of artists, film-makers and musicians (most famously The Velvet Underground), all gathered together under the loose umbrella of blankness that was Andy Warhol, one of the most successful artists of the twentieth century, who went from selling paintings of soup cans in the 1960s to being friends with Duran Duran in the 1980s. Beck recalls looking at a Velvet Underground album as a kid when his mother came over and saying, '"I know them". She was involved with Warhol, very briefly, as a dancer... She grew up in New York, on the streets.' According to Beck, who may have been exaggerating, Bibbe Hansen didn't go to school but just 'hung out with people who took drugs and she was discovered by the Factory at the age of fourteen'. Tiring of a lifestyle that a million black-clad rock groups would kill for, Bibbe Hansen moved back to Los Angeles when she was 16 and met David Campbell.

Bibbe's father and Beck's grandfather, Al Hansen, is an important part of the Beck equation. Al Hansen was an artist who came to prominence in the 1960s and was also associated with Warhol's Factory. According to his grandson, Al Hansen literally collided with the feminist Valerie Solanas, founder of the Society for Cutting Up Men (SCUM), as she left the Factory after shooting and nearly fatally wounding Andy Warhol (and thereby inspiring both a piece of art by Hansen and the Lou Reed song 'Andy's Chest'). Hansen was also associated with the much more interesting (because somewhere in there was a sense of humour, rather than a sense of eyeliner) art group Fluxus, the slightly less controversial but equally mind-stretching group of artists who included Yoko Ono. (In later life, Ono was to recall Al's work with some fondness and a Fluxus reunion enabled Beck to revisit pieces of his grandad's art that he and his brother used to, literally, trip over in their home.)

Beck tends to play down Al Hansen's role in his career – perhaps because Al never made any records and Beck rarely makes collages from discarded Hershey Bar wrappers, an Al Hansen specialty – but this is probably because Al loomed so large in Beck's life. Al taught the infant Beck the lines 'Pull down your pants/And do the hot dog dance' which were to appear much later in one of Beck's own songs. (Lyrically, Beck, whose first words on stage – in an elementary school play – were 'The donkey goes eeyore', has changed little in his couplet-obsessed rhyming style.)

If Beck's maternal grandfather was an unusual figure of one kind, his paternal grandfather was an unusual figure of another. Beck's father David Campbell was the son of a Canadian Presbyterian minister, whose travels meant that David was raised in Seattle and New York, and whose vocation meant that

Beck himself, when farmed out to grandparents, spent a lot of time in church in Kansas, absorbing influences and ambience normally not within the purview of a Los Angeles high school dropout. Kansas, apart from being the tedious home of Dorothy in *The Wizard Of Oz*, is a big, dry, wheat-filled place where the Protestant faith was bound to have a powerful stronghold. For most young musicians who dabble in rural musics like blues, folk and country, the midwest is a romantic, John Steinbeck fantasy. For Beck, sitting in church every Sunday, the midwest was a reality that informed not only his traditionalist roots but also the laconic, understated nature of his work.

Just to complete (almost) the picture of a very unusual family indeed, David Campbell is himself not a dull man. When Beck was an infant, Campbell was a busker, playing bluegrass violin in the street. He would take Beck with him in a rucksack, and it is entirely possible that Beck's love of bluegrass and country comes from having it rammed into his ears from a preverbal age (although it was equally likely that it would have distressed Beck so much that he might have turned into Trent Reznor from Nine Inch Nails).

Unlike his son, however, Campbell was no post-modern folkie. His musical skills led him to play with two of the most influential (and tiresome) artists of the early 1970s, the wet-as-ditchwater acoustic troubadour James Taylor and the Brill-Building-songwriter-turned-Me-Generation-singer Carole King, whose album *Tapestry* summed up every hippie's feelings on turning 30 and sent sales of flower pattern frocks through the roof. Campbell became King's string arranger and then went on to become an extremely popular and prolific string arranger with everyone from Neil Diamond to Bob Dylan. He also has the distinction of being one of the musicians on Marvin Gaye's astonishingly sexy *Let's Get It On*, predating his son's later obsession with sexual R&B by a quarter of a century. In the 1990s, he became the string arranger for groups ranging from Aerosmith to Green Day.

But before Campbell's success (and possibly because of his travelling musician lifestyle), life was not easy in Beck's house. They even used to skip Christmas because the family couldn't afford to celebrate it. Beck and his brother Channing were reduced to making a cardboard Christmas tree. Beck was later to remember these Christmases, unsurprisingly, as traditional but depressing, largely because the family had no money. In some ways, Beck's early life resembles the kind parodied in the TV cartoon *South Park* with the character of Kenny, the muffled trailer-park boy whose parents have no money and who is as a consequence mocked and reviled by his middle-class schoolmates. If this is the case, then Beck's subsequent career is Kenny's Revenge.

Beck's early life taught him a self-reliance unknown to most musicians, for whom women have ideally performed more of a catering than a sexual role. Beck's father would be off touring with some awful band and making them sound nice with a fat orchestra, Beck's mother would be working and there would be no-one to cook. Beck learnt to cook when he was a child, as opposed to when a TV programme or charity book approached him for his favourite recipe.

The entire family lived in a one-bedroom apartment. Beck has described the family as 'basically living in a ghetto', but is equally keen not to promote his life as some made-for-TV fairy tale. Generously, he finds wealth where others might see poverty, variety where others might see grinding monotony. It's easy to listen to Beck's varied, bric-a-brac approach to music-making and hear the voice of a man who was forced to make do with whatever he could lay his hands on, and was able to adapt and do something with it (whereas rich kids always make bad heavy metal or something equally, and appropriately, handed down by someone else who did all the work).

Beck is also in the unusual position of being able to identify with a huge section of society who lacked privilege in youth. For many musicians, a single parent family or a family left to its own devices is literally something off a poster, to be talked up at a press conference for a benefit album and then forgotten about. Beck, who, with his brother, was left to look after himself, has some empathy with the increasing amount of lone parent families in America.

This is not to say that he is a big, tiresome old liberal, banging on day in and day out about how bad his childhood was and why can't we all love each other and so on. He was also left with a healthy contempt for the idle youth of America.

'I meet fourteen-year-old kids', he once said with a degree of happy contempt, 'and they're smart asses, they think they're grown-up.'

Bibbe Hansen and David Campbell's marriage did not last. After the birth of their second son, Channing, they divorced and both Channing and Beck took their mother's surname (leading, bizarrely, to the belief among the mentally unwell in the 1990s that Beck was somehow related to blond, acne-farming brothers Hanson. Yes, that's why they spell their surnames differently, because they're related.)

Bibbe Hansen remarried and Beck's new stepfather was Sean Carrillo, a Mexican artist, into whose family Beck fitted easily. Beck maintains to this day that he feels more at ease with

Mexican people than with others. Possibly this is because at a time in his adolescence when he might have wanted a centre in his life, he got one – an instant family and an eccentric, but warm, environment.

The introduction of a Mexican family into Beck's life brought new cultural input, too. An influence on a more obvious level was the introduction of Spanish into Beck's vocabulary, both spoken and musical, from the 'Soy un perdador' chorus of 'Loser' to *Odelay's* misheard title, and in the Mariachi and acoustic party elements of his music, all factors which would enable Beck to disprove the dull MTV slacker criticisms that followed his early success.

Meanwhile, Bibbe and Sean, never ones for an easy or quiet life, opened an eaterie, the Troy Café, which quickly became an artistic centre and a focus for local bohemians in Los Angeles. As, in fact, did their home, which soon filled up with boho types, from punks and hippies to artists and, presumably, the odd hobo. It was a chaotic environment for a growing boy but it had the great advantage of introducing Beck to a huge variety of people and artistic ideas. While his schoolmates were saluting flags and learning that London, England, is not in France, Beck was absorbing the whole wide world virtually at first hand.

Unsurprisingly, Beck was not enjoying his school years at nearby Belmont Junior High. Not just because of its educational inferiority to his home environment, but because it was a violent and foul place. Beck later claimed that it was the first school in the city with airport security detectors at the doors. He was also the only white child in his neighbourhood, something he said that he did not have a problem with but clearly some other people did. He was chased by kids with lead pipes on a daily basis. Again, while other musicians boast of their supposed toughness, Beck was involved in real-life day-to-day violence, which definitely did not leave him feeling like a macho man. He later claimed that the experience made him tougher and, perhaps with a touch of irony, the fastest runner in his neighbourhood. Beck, maybe wisely, decided to drop out of school. One of his few regrets is that he had no college education; then again, he's never particularly needed any (and who wants to wear a big shirt with a stupid letter on it and live in a wooden house with ten dickweeds who think they're John Belushi but refuse to overdose anyway?).

Living in the reality of Mall America, Beck clearly has never found it funny or ironic. And, despite his fondness for eclectic music, easy listening, sci-fi films and general old tat, he has never felt comfortable with the plastic, tacky, fun world of modern America. In interviews, he likes to point out how, in the country music of the 1940s, the place most mentioned in songs was the dance joint of the day, the honky tonk, and how in the 1950s the focal point was the local hop. Now, however, the point of reference, particularly in California, is the shopping mall.

Beck, as one might guess, does not like shopping malls. Possibly because they bring back bad, violent memories. He even sounds like someone's dad as he suggests that video games are to blame, pointing out how they were once quite innocuous (early technology being so primitive that nothing more life-threatening than computer ping pong was possible) and now they are violent and hyper-realistic. Beck is worried by this sort of thing, especially with its effect on children, and finds it rather frightening. Whether or not you agree with his idea that the world is becoming a worse place because of arcade games, it's an unusual position for a fairly young pop star to take (most of his pop star peers are either sponsored by computer games manufacturers or spend every minute of their spare time playing on the wretched things).

His adolescence was not a musically significant time for Beck Hansen. Too young to absorb the 1970s influences all around him – he described the era for him as 'Blondie and Devo' – Beck was making his own musical world. He was an early, and unironic, lounge music fan, obsessed with easy listening. While everyone else was gearing up to have their clothes and record collection mocked in *The Wedding Singer*, Beck was one of the few kids on his block to own records by Henry Mancini and Antonio Carlos Jobim. He wasn't being ironic, he actually really liked Henry Mancini and Antonio Carlos Jobim.

Again, this strand in Beck's music combines with his real fondness for a kind of music otherwise mostly favoured by fake idiots in fake 1970s suits and creates a strange, relaxed core to some of his more bizarre musical excursions.

Easy listening also provided a useful contrast to another aspect of Beck's musical development. By now, both his grandfather Al and his mother had become interested in punk rock. Before he finally left America for Cologne, Al was regularly visiting punk clubs, as LA's only 50-year-old, punk-obsessed performance artist, whereas Bibbe used to let local punks crash out at the family home, and even joined local band Black Fag (not to be confused with humourless male punk group Black Flag) with local legend Vaginal Creme Davis. All this, not unnaturally, had an effect on Beck, who would come down to breakfast to find his lounge had turned into what looked like a terrorist attack on the cast of *Sid And Nancy*. Beck has memorably described his family's overnighting guests as looking like 'thrashed parrots'. His mother also claims that, on several occasions, Darby Crash spent the night on their sofa. (Germs singer Darby Crash was the LA equivalent of Johnny Rotten and Sid Vicious, a charismatic punk pioneer who died young, and having him sleep on your sofa was the 1977 LA equivalent of having a bed in 16th century England with a QUEEN ELIZABETH SLEPT HERE plaque nailed to it).

Despite having the most influential punk rock figure in the city snoring yards away from his Cheerios, Beck did not become an actual punk (not middle-class enough). Punk as a musical form has always had an arm's length influence for Beck, who was more affected by its developments in the 1980s into weirder forms of music, but punk as an attitude is clearly part of Beck's make-up, as even now he retains a Kurt Cobainish attitude to stardom, MTV and commercialism (he is one of the few American rock stars to have turned down beer ad money and seems to have sold his $1.3 million dollar house out of pure embarrassment, especially when people started describing its lush woody 1970s decor as 'Ice Storm West').

Most significantly of all in musical terms, in his teens Beck came across an album by the delta blues singer, Mississippi John Hurt. Hurt was typical of a whole group of blues musicians who had recorded and played in the 1930s, enjoying little financial reward in the overtly racist music industry of the time. Fortunately, Hurt was just one of many blues singers who was rediscovered in the blues/folk boom of the late 1950s and early 1960s, when a desire for 'authenticity' and 'roots' music among new young fans and musicians (early, R&B-obsessed bands like The Rolling Stones and Eric Clapton) enabled these blues musicians, many now in their 60s, to make records and tour again, often to larger, more appreciative white audiences than ever before.

Hurt's qualities of directness and emotional truth connected instantly with Beck, who was already well aware of how good, and bad, music could be at its most basic and acoustic. Beck found the music to be amazing. He admired its purity and heartfeltness. Significantly, he has also compared Hurt with the hippie folkies of the 1960s and 70s, whom he must have met about a million of in his youth, as they sat about either in his front room or on his dad's busking turf, warbling on about love and flowers and generally doing nothing for the world except inspire Beck's unusually venomous 'Nitemare Hippy Girl'. Mississippi John Hurt was authentic, and authentic was what Beck valued then and values now. (Even now, Hurt's 'He's A Mighty Good Leader' surfaces in Beck's live repertoire and was recorded by Beck on *Stereopathetic Soul Manure*).

Beck took up the acoustic guitar and played in much the same way that Lazarus took up his bed and walked. Like every teenage wannabe rock guitarist, he spent six months in his bedroom learning to master the instrument. Unlike every other teenage wannabe rock star, however, Beck was learning acoustic blues guitar, a skill unlikely to make him the new Eddie Van Halen. This marks him out from almost any other American or British pop star of the past twenty years. Where most people just add another layer to the crusty old mess of blues-derived rock that just gets louder and more polished with each generation, Beck was going back to, if not his, then someone else's roots. Beck was connecting, not with some mall rat's idea of a 1970s rock guitarist's idea of Jimmy Page or Eric Clapton's idea of how Muddy Waters or Sonny Boy Williamson interpreted the delta blues, but with the source. Beck at this point wasn't even listening to electric blues, the version of delta blues apparently developed by Muddy Waters in order to be audible in the crowded blues clubs of Chicago.

If Mississippi John Hurt was too obscure for the average rocker wannabe, Beck was also deeply into Koerner, Ray & Glover, a folk trio from Minneapolis. Beck, like every 1960s guitar fan, would sit down in the musty darkness of his room and attempt to work out Koerner, Ray & Glover's songs. Interestingly, he liked the trio not because they had a brilliant name but because they were doing something different with folk music. 'They were putting this rock 'n' roll energy into it', he said later. 'That's what attracted me.'

Rock 'n' roll energy or not, Beck was an extreme purist, musically, at this stage of his career. Fortunately he lightened up later on or we'd all be listening to a 30-year-old blond white man mumbling about his po' wooden shack on the banks of the ol' Missour'; but in his mid-teens, Beck was going down some extraordinary avenues. He bought a Gibson acoustic guitar because it was the same guitar that Woody Guthrie had. Guthrie is a significant figure in many ways who resonates in several important directions through pop culture. First of all, he was a living representation of the people and the grass-roots socialism of 1930s Depression America, when the divide between rich and poor was immense, when farm workers starved in the Dust Bowl and, at least in the minds of the FBI, the American Labor Movement marched to Guthrie songs like 'This Land Is Your Land'. Guthrie's left-wing populist songs were simple, direct and emotive, and have endured so well that in the 1970s Guthrie's son Arlo became the first musician's kid to become a major star with his movie and album *Alice's Restaurant*, and even now the Wilco and Billy Bragg collaborations, *Mermaid Avenue* and *Mermaid Avenue II*, with songs written up from previously unseen Guthrie lyrics, have a massive following.

Most significantly, the young Bob Dylan chose to, literally, sit at Woody Guthrie's feet, adopting his hero's hobo-in-workshirt look down to the last button and spending hours sitting next to Guthrie's bed as the singer lay dying in hospital. Dylan, who would later become an apolitical surrealist, gained all the momentum of his early career as a super-serious left-wing folkie not so much influenced by Woody Guthrie as living inside his personality like a woodpecker in a tree. What Guthrie offered to Dylan, as well as Beck, was a sense of the authentic. You could never accuse Guthrie (as you could later Dylan) of being a fraud, not in those dusty dungarees and with that beat-up guitar. (Naturally this image would rebound on Guthrie posthumously, with people who saw no humour in him, never heard his children's songs or the vaguely salacious one he wrote about Ingrid Bergman.)

Beck, who sadly never wrote THIS MACHINE KILLS FASCISTS on his Gibson acoustic like Guthrie did, appreciated Woody Guthrie for the same reasons that he loved Mississippi John Hurt: honesty, directness and emotional impact. Plus, perhaps, he could play and write songs like these two artists as well. Around this time, he began busking on buses, making up lyrics about 'Axl Rose and the levee and bus passes and strychnine', already, if you want to go over the top about references, blending surrealism and daftness with allusions to the blues and violent death.

Later, Beck was to relate Guthrie's attitude and ideals directly to his own life. He pointed out, using a knowledge of history not available to most people in rock, and remarkable for someone who dropped out of junior high, that in the 1930s, with people being forced from their homes, with the economy in freefall and vast areas of farmland devastated by the ecological disaster of the Dust Bowl, people weren't organising to help their fellow man, they were feeding on each other. In this context, Beck said, it was extraordinary to see someone like Woody Guthrie saying, 'All men are my brothers' without being overly idealistic.

Beck was able to relate to this attitude. For a start, he was poor. He was also a nice guy, as were the people who surrounded him. And with homelessness rife in America, he was able to see that the lessons of Woody Guthrie had not been learned. Very soon, he was going to be able to see this at very close quarters indeed.

In 1987, after visiting Al Hansen in Germany at Al's own art home, the Ultimate Akademie, Beck and his then girlfriend decided to cross America on a Greyhound bus to visit New York. As well as being a cheap way to travel, it positively reeked of John Steinbeck-style symbolism and the 1930s hobo tradition. Beck abandoned the Greyhound and found himself hitching, sneaking onto other buses, hiding from lunatics and generally making it to New York the very hard way.

He arrived in New York with $8 in his pocket and a guitar and that was it. In a slightly unsupportive gesture, Beck's girlfriend promptly left him. Most future rock stars would, at this point, either have burst into tears or phoned home for money. Beck still had his guitar and began playing in parks and at open-mike nights in clubs. Musically, he had come to New York at a good time. Where Los Angeles was still pretty much a poodle-metal and punk town whose greatest years were either behind it (psychedelia, surf music) or still to come (gangsta rap), New York was still maintaining its ancient tradition of being artsy on a local level and aggressive in an accessible and somehow friendly way. There was a thriving live scene, hundreds of bands and, fortunately for Beck's ears, not much actual rock. Instead, the most interesting local scene was something known as anti-folk, a reaction against the stranglehold of traditional, hippyish folk clubs in the city still unable to get over the fact that Bob Dylan and Joan Baez had played a lot in Greenwich Village in 1961.

Anti-folk was, like folk, a basic, simplistic kind of music. Unlike folk, it looked forward as well as back, and incorporated both punk and hip hop, the latter music being something that Beck had already related to as being like the blues. Beck fitted into this scene as he had previously fitted into nothing else. The great advantage of the city, Beck recalled later, was that people flowed through it like a great folkie river. Someone said about Paris that if you sit outside a café long enough, you will see everyone you know (having tried this, the author advises that this is true, but it will take up to 40,000 years for it to happen). New York is more prone to this effect, especially if one is a musician, holding a guitar and sitting in Greenwich Village or Alphabet City. Beck stayed in the same place, holding a guitar, and for the first time in his musician's life, began to meet people. A lot of people, who wanted him to play with them, who were interested in his ideas. Beck, unwittingly but willingly, became part of what was later known as 'anti-folk'.

Beck has since described anti-folk as being a very aggressive kind of folk played with punk rock energy. The sole instruments were the acoustic guitar and the human voice, both handled with more enthusiasm and verve than technical skill. For someone with Beck's attitude, this was a godsend. He could play the acoustic guitar, he was steeped in folk music and the blues (as opposed to many of his contemporaries, who were just steeped in owning a guitar and feeling shouty), and no-one cared if he made mistakes or made a fool of himself. He was free to sing all the novelty songs he wanted, and to find out what kind of a performer he wanted to be.

It was, significantly, the 1980s, a decade which has been parodied as all Wall Street, Ronald Reagan and Michael J Fox in *Family Ties*. An era obsessed with dressing in tight clothes and artificial fabrics, with hair moved from on the shoulders to on the top of the head, and characterized by coldness and ambition. Greed was good, and so were A Flock Of Seagulls. This was not going to be Beck's decade. Nevertheless, he found a place in it, with his New York musician friends. He could go into a club, and people would actually talk to him, invite him to play with them, and applaud when they were his audience. This would not have been the case in Los Angeles at the time. New York in the 1980s was the home of *Wall Street* (the film as well as the street; for obvious geographical reasons, Wall Street has always been in New York) but was also still rough enough and bohemian enough to present an alternative to Reagan's America. Los Angeles was very keen not to be an alternative to anything.

New York's local music had some effect on Beck. Once again, Warhol's Factory was influencing a Hansen's life. This time, Beck wasn't following in his mother's footsteps and being in art films. He was absorbing the influence of the Velvet Underground, whom he admired a lot, citing both the visceral sound of their records and the way they blended great tunes with huge crashing raw noise. Most of all, Beck admired the Velvets for the fact that they took their music seriously but did not take themselves seriously. 'With the Velvet Underground,' he said later, 'there was a mixture of tenderness and irony'.

Developing his own mixture of tenderness and irony – and

describing himself as a mixture of Woody Guthrie and radical rapper KRS-1 – he made his first recording of sorts, the cassette-only *Banjo Story*. Oddly unreleased by any record company at the time or since, *Banjo Story* gets its name from one of the two instruments used in its recording (the other being the acoustic guitar) and features songs like 'Going Nowhere Fast', 'Detonate', 'Farmboy', 'Breakdown' and 'Bottle Of Wine', whose titles already indicate a very Beck-like mixture of down-home rural imagery and laconic punk rock nihilism.

Around this time, Beck also recorded a couple of other tapes, the banjo and harmonica-dominated *Golden Feelings*, and *Fresh Meat And Old Slabs. Golden Feelings* was to appear later officially, but *Fresh Meat And Old Slabs* was not, being material Beck recorded for his mother's birthday. It has, however, been extensively bootlegged because it contains primitive attempts at the likes of 'Loser', 'Satan Gave Me A Taco' and the wonderfully-named 'Steve Threw Up'.

Beck also began to introduce one of his later trademarks into his act, as he started to appear on stage wearing a *Star Wars* stormtrooper mask (a Beck obsession which would have surfaced in the 'Loser' video had not the generous and humour-filled Lucasfilm company decided not to allow Beck to use their mask).

Unlike George Lucas, Beck is now over *Star Wars*, despite (or perhaps because of) seeing the film forty times. But life at this time, *Star Wars* masks and primitive tapes and all, was not fun. The initial bohemian euphoria was tempered with the realities of street life. Walking around New York with a guitar marked Beck out, in the eyes of muggers and scum, as a rich kid. He was mugged frequently. This was a depressing period in a life which so far had had few high points. Kenny's Revenge was a long way off. Beck, however, appears to have the kind of temperament which remains unaffected by life's little ups and downs. He said of this time, 'If you ask anybody that knows me, they'll tell you that I've had just the worst fucking luck.' (In retrospect, it was probably inevitable that Beck's first single was going to be called 'Loser'.) On more than one occasion, Beck has been a little more specific about the romance of street life. Despite the camaraderie and excitement of his life, he was still officially homeless, still walking the streets in the hope of seeing someone he knew, finding himself in a very cold city in winter, and worst of all, being mugged so badly that he was hospitalized. Ultimately, Beck's life in New York was unromantic, as real suffering always is.

In the end, New York and Beck seem to have exhausted one another in different ways, so Beck returned to Los Angeles. He began to drift through jobs and homes, unloading trucks, working as a hot dog man at kids' parties, sleeping at the homes of various family members and in a variety of rooming houses. He continued to play shows and would often sit in with a friend's band. The friend was Steven Hanft, later Beck's video collaborator, and the band were called Loser. Part of Loser's show involved Beck emerging from a coffin like Screamin' Jay Hawkins playing horrible guitar. (This would be around the time that Beck would invariably claim he only listened to 'devil-worshipping' heavy metal band Slayer.)

To support himself, Beck worked as a sign painter and, in a move which only in Beck's career would have ramifications later, became one of those men who come to your garden, armed with a large leaf-eating vacuum cleaner. Beck clearly became affectionate towards leaf-blowers while he was doing this job, and on many occasions since has employed them onstage, both for their brilliance as noise makers and for their symbolic effect of blowing people away. (Beck seems to be obsessed with horticultural equipment in a weird way – one of his spoken-word, or rather mumbled-word, tracks, '8.4.82', makes enthusiastic reference to stealing another great gardening tool, the Weed Whacker.)

Around this time Beck met his long-term girlfriend, Leigh Limon. Significantly, they met in a second-hand clothes store. Ever since Beck became well known, every interview he has ever done has focused at bizarre length on what Beck – styled by Leigh – is wearing (a trait that Beck would later acknowledge in an awards acceptance speech). Apart from her beauty, personality and ability to choose Beck-type clothing, an important fact about Limon for Beck is that 'she knew me when I was a penniless nothing. She liked me long before anybody else did. And that's important.'

Where before New York, Beck had been a loner playing in his bedroom and a local white boy getting chased by black kids, after his return to LA he was a real musician, part of a local scene. Just as The Beatles were able to come back to their native Liverpool from Hamburg changed for ever, so Beck was a changed man after his experiences in New York. He was older, better-travelled, and full of new ideas. Now he was playing shows with local musicians, just as he had done in New York. (At one show, legend has it, Mike Tyson got onstage in a Santa Claus hat and pissed on the drum kit. No-one knows why, but it sounds like a very public cry for help.) When not having his drums lubricated by Iron Mike, Beck also appeared in a documentary about the Los Angeles poetry scene. More importantly, he made his first proper recording.

One day in August 1991, Beck was playing the Sunset

Junction Street Fair in Los Angeles and one of the people in the audience – or, to be more honest, one of the people walking past Beck as he performed – was Rob Schnapf, who was one of the bosses of a record label called Bong Load Custom. A week later, in one of the coincidences that infest any localized music scene, Beck was playing at the nearby Jabberjaw club and this time was heard by Rob Schnapf's partner Tom Rothrock. Rothrock and Schnapf compared notes, realized they were talking about the same person, and then Rothrock introduced Beck to rap producer Carl Stephenson. Stephenson had not worked with anyone like Beck before. In fact, he had worked with The Geto Boys, an aggressive, early gangsta rap act.

Beck went round to Stephenson's home. After a shaky start – Beck thinks he remembers Stephenson actually walking out of the room – they recorded 'Loser' on the spot, Stephenson being particularly impressed with Beck's riff for the song. In a few short hours, in Carl Stephenson's lounge, Beck Hansen's career was born. As is often the case with imminent fame, everything started to happen at once. Having never made a record, Beck had now made two, the other being the infamous 'MTV Makes Me Want To Smoke Crack' on the Flipside label. In January 1993 the *Golden Feelings* tape came out on Sonic Enemy and then in March, Bong Load released 'Loser'.

'Loser' made Beck an instant star. Pedants will point out that Beck had been playing and making tapes for years, but the fact remains that 'Loser' was the first actual record he'd ever released, and, as it remains the only independent record ever to go top ten in the USA, it seems reasonable to remark that it was 'Loser', and not, say, the *Golden Feelings* tape that marked Beck's debut on the public stage. Beck credits 'Loser' for his success but remains modest about the whole thing. He likes to point out that, as he began his career playing folk music, there was no chance of him having any degree of commercial success, but when he recorded 'Loser', he suddenly became a commercial property, and since then people have stayed with him to see what he's going to do next. True, but people seem to have stayed with Beck for an awfully long time on the off-chance that he's going to do something commercial, and on several occasions they have given him all their money to do something utterly uncommercial.

In a similar vein, he explained that having worked in a traditional vein for a very long time, he decided to be a little more experimental. Beck claims that he enjoyed the response to 'Loser'. His metaphor is, naturally, an artistic one. He compares his early work to someone sketching with a pencil and then discovering that they can paint and work in colour. Once Beck was out of the folk cave, and a world of possibilities opened up, he found it hard to go back (and if 'Loser' is just painting in colour, then *Odelay* must be spray paint and *Midnite Vultures* must be a graffiti artist gone mad. Possibly.)

'Loser' was a huge hit for two reasons. One, it was, and is, a brilliant single, a hilarious lyric tied to a unique sound. Two, it seemed to tap into a new social phenomenon, the slacker. No-one knows if there ever were any real 'slackers' and, if so, how they differed from the more traditional 'middle class lazy people' of before, but Beck's indolent, insolent and witty song – 'I'm a loser baby/ So why don't you kill me?' – seemed to sum it all up. Naturally, Beck has disliked the term 'slacker' ever since he heard it. In interview after interview, it is the topic that he returns to (or is made to return to) time and time again.

Here, condensed and blended from a thousand interviews, are the Top Five reasons why Beck dislikes being crowned King of the Slackers.

1) 'Loser' isn't about apathy or not caring as a fashion statement. The lyric is Beck talking about the fact that he is not a very good rapper.
2) The whole thing is a coincidence. Beck made 'Loser' at a time when the 'slacker' concept was very trendy indeed and everyone just assumed he was commenting on the zeitgeist.
3) 'Loser' is not about slackers, it's about misfits. Slackers opt out of society, misfits are never part of it. 'Loser' is a song about someone who doesn't fit into society and isn't bothered by it. It's an anti-hero song. Here the lines are severely blurred.
4) Beck is not a slacker himself. His central disassociation from slackerdom is a class-based or income-based one. He was never one of the well-off kids who, having nothing to struggle against, just get bored and sulky about life. And, unlike someone's dad who uses his early years of struggle as a hammer to bore future generations with, Beck has not been soured by his financially-deprived childhood. He's an outsider, but not a whiny one with his baseball cap on backwards.
5) Beck is active. Slackers are passive. Beck has always been doing stuff, whether it's travelling, making music or just sucking leaves up for money. Slackers are, aptly, the MTV Generation because all they do is watch MTV. If the remote was faulty, they would just as easily become the Discovery Generation or the Financial Channel Generation.

In the end, slackerdom went away, as Beck knew it would. Not for him a career as the Liberace of slackers, condemned forever to come on stage with a slacker piano and a slacker candelabra and reminiscing about the good old days watching *Clerks* with Beavis and Butthead and getting sores from sitting on old Dorito chips for a month. But one side effect of slackerdom that Beck could not have anticipated was the corporate one. Correctly guessing that if slackers existed, then they would sit on their behinds and drink beer all day, Budweiser offered Beck over a hundred thousand dollars to use 'Loser' as music in one of their ad campaigns. Beck refused, an attitude admirable for a man who had been working for $4 an hour.

But then, Beck, unusually in pop music, is a modest man. He sees even 'Loser' as a chance combination of circumstances, a chain of events that is utterly random, from being phoned up and asked to go to Carl Stephenson's house, from going down and finding Stephenson with a drum machine and eight-track, to them getting together to make 'Loser'. Beck claims that instead he could have just as easily gone out and had a drink with a friend and none of this would ever have happened and as a result, presumably, he would still be sucking leaves off lawns and thinking, 'Nah, I could never have made it'.

This is a modest nonsense of a theory. For a start, unless he had got so drunk with his imaginary beer friend, Beck would have carried on doing shows in the local area and sooner or later would have been approached by someone else from a record company. He might never have written 'Loser', but chances are he might have written another of the 400 or so songs he has composed since then, many of which have been quite commercial in their own right. And even the going-for-beer theory is flawed, since Beck has always been the king practitioner of the Bohemian Work Ethic. Chance, his ass.

Now that he had finally been noticed by the big world of music, Beck's next move was not, as the record companies and breweries now circling his career hoped, to release an album called *Look At All These Songs Like Loser* with follow-up singles 'Slacker', 'Let's Do The Slack' and 'Loser Twist'. Instead he stepped aside, career-wise, and made *One Foot In The Grave*, a low-key, country-flavoured album, with his musician friend (from the group Beat Happening) Calvin Johnson.

*One Foot In The Grave*, with its title alluding both to country-death songs and to Beck's old-before-his-time musical ethic, was recorded in less than a week in Calvin Johnson's cellar. Johnson's home is some way from Los Angeles, in a small town called Olympia up in Washington state, which according to Beck is a hive of activity for many punk rock groups, the most famous of whom are almost all-girl rockers Bikini Kill. (Unlikely as it may seem, Beck claims that Olympia was the cradle of the entire Riot Grrrl movement).

Johnson found Beck's music emotionally affecting, so affecting in fact that when two or three years previously Beck gave him a tape of some songs that Beck had recorded, Johnson started to cry. Presumably he was not crying in pain, as the duo resolved to work together. They went into Johnson's cellar and recorded thirty or more songs, which Johnson then whittled down to fifteen for the album.

Beck later accurately described the album as a mixture of folk and country. He summed up *One Foot In The Grave*'s unique musical blend as being 'acoustic hardcore, with cardboard drums'. *One Foot In The Grave* also features Beck's own version of his hero Mississippi John Hurt's 'He's A Mighty Good Leader'.

The album also features a Johnny-Cash style duet with Johnson, who is blessed with a very deep voice indeed, a few acoustic songs, the odd loud blues number, and what Beck describes as 'a pretty little '60s thing, called "Asshole".' This title Beck apparently finds both amusing and also something of an allusion. As a title, 'Asshole' is a particular Beck cornerstone relating, by the way, to one of his favourite groups, the cultish and terrifying Pussy Galore. Beck likes to tell people as they gather round his knee, grandchild-like, how Pussy Galore had a song called 'Asshole' as well as one called 'Pig Sweat' and one called 'Fucker'. Golden memories of misty-eyed youth.

Beck also signed to the mighty Geffen organization, a move flavoured with some irony. David Geffen had begun his career signing what future generations will recall as the most horrible of LA acts, the so-called Laurel County aristocracy of Linda Ronstadt and The Eagles, and made them into enormous soft-rock successes. Doing this helped the growth of country rock, a hybrid music that blended contemporary rock with dope-addled country music, in a way that Beck never would (ie, badly).

In the 1990s, David Geffen was reinventing himself as a cooler, more contemporary figure. Things had, however, started rather badly when Geffen found himself in dispute with music business maverick Neil Young, after Young's most recent albums had not performed as well as Geffen had hoped, and the label had accused Young of recording 'unrepresentative' music. (This action in turn decided R.E.M. against signing with Geffen and, R.E.M. legend has it, prompted Young to say to Geffen, 'Heard about you and them Reem boys... ') Beck went with Geffen, but had a clause in his contract permitting him to release uncommercial records, by implication on Bong Load.

Beck was keen to assert his independence to the press. He told interviewers that he did what he wanted. He denied the existence of record company pressure, saying that the only pressure he felt as a recording artist was from himself. Clearly he is either barking mad, or Beck has actually managed to sign a deal which does give him the freedom he needs to work. (Certainly the appearance of the unfunky *Stereopathetic Soul Manure* would indicate the latter.)

Beck would respond badly as an artist if asked to churn records out of a similar nature on a yearly basis. He claimed at the time, as he would rightly claim now, that his work has a spontaneous nature to it.

When *Odelay* was released, Beck pointed out that he never plans projects in advance, claiming that things have a tendency to just turn up without him expecting them to (as a theory, this certainly explains the spontaneous nature of his recording work). He also expressed the urge to put together an album of out-takes from *Odelay*, which would be more like his conventional, if that's the right word, songs, without the hip hop backing.

Beck, as a musician, swings like a pendulum do. Obvious though it is to note, Beck likes to go from danceable to folky, from country to hip hop. If he makes a record which reeks of the sampled drum, he will tire of that sound and go round the block again and make an acoustic album. Then, sickened by the chime of the guitar, he longs for hip hop again. And the fact that, while his dance crossover records make pots of wad for Geffen, his stranger, more introverted guitar music does not seems to bother Beck very little. Releasing uncommercial records is, logically, commercial suicide (although Beck's uncommercial records sell better than most people's commercial ones). Beck seems more concerned with longevity.

He tells reporters that he's not particularly concerned with the fleeting nature of popularity because popularity is, by definition, fleeting. Beck sees himself as a folk artist carrying on a long tradition. Folk music is timeless. Beck wants, clearly, to be part of that strand. One of the reasons he hated the slacker tag, possibly, is because it set him in an era and isolated him from the flow of music. Beck hated being the flavour of the month, a situation he memorably described as 'a postcard from somewhere, not a place you live'.

Although very clear on the issue of longevity, perhaps sensibly, when asked about the contents of his major label record deal, Beck immediately turns into the inscrutable Bob Dylan of *Blonde On Blonde*, saying 'I got some strawberries, some blueberries, a haysack, a silver spacesuit'. He went into the studio and recorded his debut album proper, the easy-listening-titled *Mellow Gold*, whose release prompted the reissue of 'Loser'. *Mellow Gold* was an instant hit, its mixture of styles probably surprising a few people, but most appreciating the versatility, humour and dryness of Beck's world.

Beck is still not completely happy with *Mellow Gold*. He talked at the time in a seemingly nostalgic way about the spontaneous nature of the project, working with Carl Stephenson, mixing up rap and folk and dance music. He even gave journalists a thumbnail description of Carl's previous act, The Geto Boys, whom he described, tongue mating with cheek, as hardened criminals who wrote songs about killing people and cutting them into pieces (perhaps this is a slightly pointed reference to Stephenson's sudden disdain for the apparent negativity of 'Loser').

Beck then goes on to claim that *Mellow Gold* was a rough affair that could have done with a bit more work, more acoustic songs and country songs that might have been more representative of his work at the time. He also suggested that the thrust of *Mellow Gold* was in fact related to trying to get it finished before Stephenson's girlfriend came home to make herself dinner. As Beck and Carl were working in Carl's living room-cum-diner area, they would have to stop recording so Carl's girlfriend could eat. This meant, bizarrely, that large parts of *Mellow Gold* were put together by two grown men trying to make sure that they had cleared out of the kitchen before tea time. (This would never have happened in England; there, the whole thing would have been done in a shed at the bottom of the garden.)

However, anyone thinking of buying *Mellow Gold* and worrying that the man who made it does not like it need not fret too much. First of all, the people who make records are not always the best judges of their work (as anyone will know who's ever read an interview with some tired old rocker who claims his new record is 'the best of my career'. And hearteningly, recently Beck claims to have heard *Mellow Gold* again and to have found it 'not bad.'

He toured the world promoting 'Loser' and *Mellow Gold* and, in a stunt that Yoko Ono, Andy Warhol and Beck's grandad Al would have appreciated, performed 'Loser' on Britain's most important chart TV show, *Top Of The Pops*, with a band comprised totally of old men because, he said at the time, he knew the show's producers appreciate old men. Perhaps he thought the show's name meant Top Of The Old Fathers. Beck also confessed to hiring the old man from the Benny Hill Show playing the drums, whom they had to send home to prevent him dying as he was 98. (Presumably, the urge to rap on the old man's bald head Benny Hill-style must have been almost irresistible.)

The old men themselves would probably have appreciated Beck's other album of the year, *Stereopathetic Soul Manure*, whose more considered, more insane nature brought mixed reviews from people not yet used to Beck and which enabled him to establish himself as Mister Not Always Pop.

Beck points out that *Stereopathetic Soul Manure* features several of his oldest songs as well as more recent material. Oddly, the newest songs were the most traditional, with their pedal steel and other country elements. The way to tell a really old Beck song, he revealed, is if it has something of a novelty element. A tune like 'Satan Gave Me A Taco' is so old that it goes back to Beck's days as a folk club singer playing in cafés, where the only way to keep the folk-sated, acoustically-drained audience awake was to improvise daft songs just to keep them from nodding off into their carrot cake.

There was an element of country nostalgia in *Stereopathetic Soul Manure*, possibly inspired by meeting a homeless person called Ken, a former country singer who sings on the record, and also by Beck's own country past. He claims that a few years back he had actually had a country group who played once a week in a hotel in a little town up in the mountains. Their repertoire consisted entirely of oldies by Hank Williams, Jimmie Rodgers and George Jones, and they bolstered up the set with folk, accompanied on fiddle and banjo. The audience did not, as normally happens in these kinds of story, leap up and down and shout, 'You are the future of country music!' but sat there eating steak and fries. 'It was pretty funny,' said Beck later.

*Stereopathetic Soul Manure*, for Beck, represents his past and in particular influences like the blues of Hurt and country roots singers like the Carter Family. It could just as easily have become a trad niche for Beck in the way that, in a different direction, slackerdom might have been. However, Beck is no fool. He had already become aware that there are dangers in shackling oneself to traditional music. In this he was somewhat prophetic, as the recent alt.country movement has shown. Much of alt.country is great, but a lot of it is student twaddle, youngsters from good homes pretending that they are drifting cowboys, using only beat-up guitars, dressing like Woody Guthrie on a bad dungaree day and generally making the Amish look like the Jetsons. Beck refused to live in someone else's past, to, in his own words, 'eternally do things as if it was 1932' and thus was led away from rural hippy trails into a new kind of music. Thank God, eh?

With a wealth of new material to perform, Beck continued to tour and, like an incontinent golden goose, also managed to bring out yet another record, this time the 10-inch vinyl release *A Western Harvest Field By Moonlight*. In 1994, Beck was prolific, he was tired, and he was famous. '1994 hasn't been very kind to me. People very quickly came to a very false image of me,' he moaned like an old daddy. Having become well known for something he was not – an idle, cynical middle-class boy who made folk-rap records – he was now expected to go and tour and promote something that he wasn't.

Beck's career in the wider world also coincided with a bad time for American live music. The grunge scene that had been so exciting and new a few years ago was now moribund. Events like Lollapalooza had become generic rock festivals, with little of the resigned exuberance and mud-happy good nature that characterized their European counterparts. Beck, now touring with a full-on band behind him, found himself playing to bored audiences again. This time, though, the audiences were not bored because they hadn't heard of him, they were just bored full stop, in that spoiled rock fan way, where if you don't give people what they want, they will go crazy for it, but when you do give it to them, they suck their thumbs and throw plastic cups.

Beck's memory of 1995 can be summed up in a phrase he used to describe his festival experiences. 'What comes to mind?' he asked himself, 'Blue plastic seats. Empty. Very empty.' And despite Courtney Love's note in her Lollapalooza diary – 'Wish Kurt could have been here to meet Beck, he would've liked him a lot' – the year was getting grimmer and grimmer. Al Hansen died, as did several of Beck's friends. 'At the time I was thinking, am I gonna write a bunch of songs about death?' said Beck later, and it's certainly true that around this period he wrote 'Dead Melodies', 'Cancelled Check' and 'Cold Brains', songs with, at best, negative themes.

However, these songs were put on hold when Beck met the two producers who for many have so far served him best – the Dust Brothers, Mike Simpson and John King. The Dust Brothers worked with semi-novelty rapper Tone-Loc (of 'Wild Thing' and 'Funky Cold Medina' fame) in the early 1990s and famously turned round the Beastie Boys' career with the genuinely influential *Paul's Boutique* album, on which they allowed the three squawking New York rich boys to boast over tracks already recorded by Simpson and King. (The Dust Brothers also achieved fame of another kind when a British DJing duo called themselves The Dust Brothers on their early records and after being sued changed their name to The Chemical Brothers and released an album called *Exit Planet Dust*).

Beck had a slightly downbeat relationship between himself and 'Loser' producer Carl Stephenson, who now apparently regrets the 'negative' nature of Loser (it's FUNNY), saying

'I feel bad about it. It's not Beck the person, it's the words. I just wish I could have been more of a positive influence'.

In contrast, the Dust Brothers and Beck got on extremely well in the studio. They listened to vast amounts of unusual records, mixed everything up, wrote together and generally created a lot of music, a mixture more eclectic even than *Mellow Gold*'s. Beck was possibly uncertain of the record's commercial potential when he told Australian journalists it was 'a beautiful way to go out, a beautiful disaster'. He was also made a little antsy by what appeared to be delays with *Odelay*'s release. He had finished the album some time before visiting Australia on tour, then he got involved in the Lollapalooza tour, where he premiered a lot of the now-ageing tracks. However, he assured the press that it was going to have 'a nice round, nutty flavor to it, a sort of walnut and cedar flavor'. And, in many ways, he's right.

The album's title, famously, is a mistranscription. Beck wanted to give one of the album's songs, 'Lord Only Knows', the title 'Órale', which is, according to Beck, 'a Mexican slang word that I grew up hearing and, uh, I didn't really know what it meant. It's a word you grow up with... you know what it means, but you never knew literally what it means. It's a word that I associate with being among friends and enjoying myself, you know.' It would have been an excellent title with good associations for Beck, but the engineer wrote it down as 'Odelay', which Beck, naturally, decided would be a good title for the album.

After *Mellow Gold* had, seemingly, confused the world, *Odelay* set the record straight and established Beck as an artist with a consistent world view and musical vision. Its production was superb, beautifully-layered and possibly only The Dust

Brothers, with their eclectic tastes and enormous knowledge of music, could have come to terms so easily with Beck's wide-ranging tastes and desire to mix them all up. Best of all for Beck, who felt one area where *Mellow Gold* was lacking was his own singing, The Dust Brothers were happy to spend almost as much time on his vocals as they did on the music tracks. This new attitude was good, as the music scene was changing, and Beck was keen to move on. When 'Loser' came out he was keen to point out that he was not a slacker. Now, on the eve of *Odelay*'s release, he was keen to point out that he wasn't 'alternative', claiming that the very word had become a synonym for 'desperate'. And for the benefit of the people who had to stock his albums, Beck also helpfully suggested a special section for *Odelay* in record stores – Hindu Trucker Goth Samba.

Now, with an album full of Hindu Trucker Goth Samba to promote, Beck returned to the road. This time round, his first tour was as a support act. Every night he was opening as an acoustic act for Sonic Youth, the New York avant-rockers whose feedback-soaked rock seemingly contrasted heavily with Beck's acoustic numbers. Then again, for a long time Beck had been friendly with Sonic Youth's leader, the conceptual punk rocker Thurston Moore. Moore was an early fan of Beck's from 'Loser' days, and his sense of humour and interest in anarchic art seem to go well with Beck's. Moore famously interviewed Beck for MTV, an occasion where Beck barely spoke, in a kind of artistic way. They were both contributors to a self-explanatory book called *The Lollapalooza '95 Tour Journals*.

Beck also appears on an album compiled by Moore on which artists were invited to contribute short (very short) guitar pieces. The album is called *Kill Any/All Spin Personnel*, a title possibly related to the time Beck did a photo session for *Spin* magazine three or four years previously. He claimed that the photographer 'airbrushed' his face and made him look 'like some Goth clown'. Beck was set on revenge and suggested putting a banana up the photographer's tail pipe, so perhaps this album title is Beck's revenge. (This after all the awards *Spin* has given Beck, too. For shame.) Beck also appeared, more sanely, on an album supporting Tibetan freedom.

In 1996, the *Odelay* tour proper began. Beck began to introduce into his performance the more theatrical elements that he is now famous for, namely stage costumes and dance moves – he is, notoriously, a very good dancer, and, as has been noted, likes to dress up, or at least be dressed up by Leigh Limon.

Beck was now coming into his own, not just as a solo musician, but as a solo artist. There is an important distinction between the two; solo musicians play stuff in subways, solo artists perform and are showmen. The three artists most similar to Beck in stage presence are David Bowie, for variety, surrealism and interest in generally subversive art statements for their own sake, Neil Young, for dogged individualism, music based in authenticity, and an odd ability to change all the time while still seeming rootsy, and Prince, for being sexy, dancing and humping a giant bed on stage.

The main motif, costume-wise, of the *Odelay* tour was Beck's country-and-western-style suit. The suit confused many of the audience, who presumably thought that Beck had been sent by The Man to make them all get real jobs and wash or something, but in fact Beck was tapping into a tradition unknown to the less active members of his audience; he was wearing a Nudie suit, one of the beautifully decorated, slightly camp and definitely over-the-top outfits made by tailor Nudie Cohen for country singers. Beck's suit, he claimed, which had been acquired originally for the purposes of making a video, had apparently been made for one of Beck's country idols, the late Gram Parsons. 'But', Beck said cheerfully, 'Most people take it for a John Travolta outfit.'

Beck wore the suit for two reasons: one, it contradicted and mocked the image he felt he had had stuck onto him of the grunge slacker kid, always wearing flannel shirts and jeans with big holes in them; and two, it paid tribute to someone he genuinely respected, but was not particularly well-known to the millions of MTV viewers and Lollapalooza visitors who by now were massively into Beck.

By namechecking Gram Parsons, Beck was also taking his place in a line of musicians who had worked in country music, loved it but done different things with it. (He was also later to duet on one of Parsons' songs, 'Sin City', with Parsons' partner and collaborator Emmylou Harris.) Just as Parsons' work harked back to the roots of country, and adapted it for a modern audience, so Beck went back to country, and without the tiresome irony of some of the college boy- (and girl-) patronising alt.country bands.

Beck has always liked country and western music, even as far back as the father of modern country, Hank Williams, who wrote exciting hoedown tunes and mournful ballads and died in the back of his own car. Beck has described Williams as one of those charismatic personalities who could make other people happy but not themselves. His favourite Hank Williams songs include the maudlin 'Lovesick Blues', the downright suicidal 'I'll Never Get Out Of This World Alive' and the ridiculous song about a wooden cigar store Indian, 'Kaw-liga'. 'I love songs about the Indians,' explained Beck.

Beck came to country on his own, as he did most other

things. He claims that when he was young, other kids would mock country music, but for Beck 'it came across as beautiful and totally serious'. He even has little time for other groups who do play country, naming no names but asserting that these groups 'were playing country, but they did it in a kind of condescending way, like they were looking down on it from above'. Beck likes country because it is direct and emotional, 'whereas in rock music everything is hidden behind irony. Country is refreshing'.

With this attitude, it was inevitable that Beck was never going to be the ironic hip slacker the media wanted him to be. His attitude to suddenly being in fashion, too, was not what the casual rock fan might expect.

Despite this, 1997 began with Beck entering the Youthful Mainstream full-on as he appeared in a sketch on *Saturday Night Live* with Michael Palin and Kevin Spacey. He then went back to taking *Odelay* around the entire known world, continuing a tour that finally ended at the Universal Amphitheater in Los Angeles, at least enabling Beck to get the tour bus to drop him off outside his front door.

In May 1997 he played again in Britain, and in June he performed an acoustic set at the Los Angeles premiere of a film called *Kill The Moonlight*. Directed by Beck's main video collaborator Steven Hanft, *Kill The Moonlight* cost $14,000 and was the film that, in many ways, inspired 'Loser'. Described at the time as 'a dark comedy that chronicles big loser Chance Strother's lame attempts to raise money to fix his broken race car', *Kill The Moonlight* also boasted, predictably and sensibly, a soundtrack album, featuring 'Loser'.

At the end of June, possibly suffering from jet lag, Beck returned to Britain to play the Glastonbury Festival. Around this time, the Miller corporation offered Beck $100,000 to use the song 'Where It's At' from *Odelay*, presumably on the grounds that Miller Beer is where it's at, and not just another straw-colored fizzy drink. As he had done with Budweiser and 'Loser' at the start of his career, Beck turned down the price of a house and the chance to be forever remembered as the man who did the music for a beer ad.

1998 began with a festival in January. Admittedly, it was in Perth (being Australia, it was called the Mudslinger Festival) and it was followed by a full tour of Australia and New Zealand. It was around this time, Beck claims, that he tried to start work on the songs and sound of *Midnite Vultures* but a computer ate one of the songs so, Beck claims now, he decided to make the very different *Mutations*. He gave his song notebook to Leigh Limon and asked her to select the songs that she liked. When she did so, Beck had the songs for his next album. Now he needed a producer. Beck had wanted for some time to work with Radiohead's producer Nigel Godrich, and things were arranged at the high levels that these things are arranged at in the music industry. Godrich flew to Los Angeles in February and spent a weekend working with Beck so the two of them could get to know one another. It went so well that one or other of them decided that they could actually make an album in two weeks. In March, Godrich and Beck did exactly that, emphasizing the deliberate, rough feel of the music and working so fast that Godrich actually left for the airport while the last track was being mixed. (Presumably Beck had now got over his fear of rough-sounding records.)

*Mutations* was released, after some legal problems concerning its 'commerciality'. Not, oddly, the expected ones – Geffen, having started off convinced that Neil Young was giving them unsaleable records, now suddenly found that Beck, from whom they'd anticipated the odd chart clunker, was making unusual records that they could sell. The new record, spooky, country-ish and at times reminiscent of Led Zeppelin's psychedelic folk, did well, although the obvious lack of a 'Where It's At' or a 'Loser', or indeed anything catchy and danceable, made it less than MTV-friendly. It is still, however, one of Beck's best albums.

In September 1998, Beck went to New York to participate in the opening of 'Playing With Matches', a collection of art by Al Hansen, which Beck and his brother Channing had also contributed to. Beck and Channing were joined by Thurston Moore, Yoko Ono and Bibbe Hansen. On the night, Ono fondly remembered Al Hansen, not least for one of his pieces, the memorably-named *Yoko Ono Piano Drop*. Many of Al Hansen's collages were displayed, made from Hershey bar wrappers, cigarette butts, and matches. Meanwhile Beck was described in the book of the exhibition as having 'a junkman's passion for discarded styles and stances', which is fair enough.

More touring took place, more awards, more recordings and even more editions of *Saturday Night Live*. *The Golden Feelings* CD was reissued and Beck's regular drummer, Joey Waronker, joined R.E.M.. Life went on in Beckworld and the world would not have been surprised if things had never changed, with Beck alternating obscurish countrified records with great big folk-rap ones. Instead, he opted for a third direction, this time working with DJ Micky Petralia and guitarist Tony Hoffer, putting together an album whose musical direction was inspired by one of Beck's old songs, 'Debra'.

The resulting album, *Midnite Vultures*, was the first Beck album to come in for a large degree of stick, even being viewed as controversial in some quarters. From its garish, 1980s disco-referential sleeve, to its unusually sexual lyrical content, *Midnite Vultures* has been viewed by some as a failed attempt to make a Rick James album for the turn of the millennium. It's actually more likely to be a pastiche of R&B and rap, musics that Beck finds fascinating, than the result of a genuinely idiosyncratic talent with a surrealist bent like Beck's involving himself in modern dance music. And at this stage in his career, for many people a Beck album that doesn't sound like what's gone before will be annoying, no matter what it sounds like.

At the time Beck pointed out that he could have done the sensible, career-rock-star thing and recorded another version of *Odelay*, which would have taken him until about lunchtime to make, but that would have been, in Beck's words, 'obvious and cheap'. And irrelevant. This time around, as at every time around, Beck knew exactly what he wanted to do. Despite being a musician who favoured variety and experiment, Beck was finding his new change of direction difficult and at times obstinate. But he was unable to give up, and in the end produced an album which no-one else could have made. 'At times it felt like we were going to hell and back on each song, but I knew what I wanted,' he said afterwards. 'I don't know if that's a blessing or a curse.'

Nevertheless, for the first time, a Beck album has come in for a critical hammering. Beck is obviously not happy at what he sees as a misinterpretation of his aims. Critics have looked at the song titles, the artwork and the general groove and taken *Midnite Vultures* at face value. Beck has been oddly vocal in his protests. He said at the time that *Midnite Vultures* wasn't designed to be, in his own words, 'a '70s disco-ball boogie thing at all'. To Beck, *Midnite Vultures* is a more subtle record, but the critics have heard a few 1980s-sounding funk riffs and vaguely salacious lyrics and decided that Beck has gone sex-funk mad. 'They hear a clav or a certain synthesizer sound and it gets relegated to Rick James Land,' Beck told *Rolling Stone*, memorably: 'I was trying to make some fun music for people who aren't a cheap audience. It has thought to it, but it's still fun. There's a lot of meaningful, intelligent music being made without fun or getting down on its mind. This is music for the body as well.'

Listening at first to *Midnite Vultures*, with its sex-o-matic riffs and pimpish boasts, the lazy comparison would be with Prince; a more accurate one might be with David Bowie, who at the height of his glam rock/weirdy spaceman period got fed up with being from the moon, became obsessed with the Philadelphia soul music that was everywhere around him, and recorded *Young Americans*. Bowie's *Young Americans* doesn't sound a lot like *Midnite Vultures*, but has one important thing in common with it; it is a completely idiosyncratic, individual album whose lyrics and themes have only loose connections to the R&B music of the day, but which would not have existed without that music.

This vague Bowie connection comes up in Beck's most recent thoughts. When asked about the continuity of his career – and at this point in his career, it's a very good question – Beck revealed that he had been giving a lot of thought to the issue. It seems he had been reading a Japanese magazine which, in the obsessively-detailed tradition of Japanese magazines, was illustrating articles about long-established artists like Neil Young or David Bowie with photos of their albums. Beck was impressed by the fact that with these artists, there would be pictures of '30 or 40' albums. This did not, as it easily could, make him suicidal, but made him realise that, essentially, he is still at the start of his career. After four albums, he claimed, he was at '*Ziggy Stardust* or *Aladdin Sane* in terms of Bowie's albums', and that he wanted to go on and emulate Bowie and Young and make his own thirty or forty albums (he did also acknowledge that maybe four or five will be his lot. He really doesn't seem to be a vain man at all, Beck).

It's clearly an issue which exercises Beck's mind a great deal. He has never been a conventional pop star and, indeed, has often avoided the trappings of pop for the slower backroads. At thirty, he is at what most musicians would call a crossroads in their careers, but instead of weeping uncontrollably and reaching for drugs and hair dye, Beck is philosophical and even forward-looking. He can remember being twenty years old and 'thinking about all the amazing musicians who come out and do a few great things, and then something happens'. Like most music fans, Beck has watched people with talent become successful and then seemingly lose all their abilities. He wonders whether these people genuinely lose their powers or whether success is simply a more interesting place for them to be. 'My dream was to go through that door and still do interesting things,' he has said.

This is a theme Beck returns to time and time again. He's even compared young musicians who lose it and then disappear to people who work in other, possibly more taxing trades, such as carpenters, who undergo a long apprenticeship and instead of going mad after they've made some cupboards and drinking all the wood polish, simply carry on working and get better and become better carpenters than they were when they were young and kept hitting their thumbs with the hammer and storming out into the yard vowing never to work with mahogany ever again. 'With music, it seems that people think the opposite is the case. I don't,' he says. 'Writing songs is an art but it's also a job. I have the feeling that I'll be better in a few years. What does a 20-year-old have to say about life?'

Beck is now entering the fourth decade of his life and his best work may well be yet to come. Maybe a period of critical disfavour is what Beck really needs; his best work has often come out of adversity – he was unknown when he made 'Loser', he was deemed to be a disappointment before *Odelay*, and now perhaps *Midnite Vultures*' less-than-warm reception will fuel a different future. Meanwhile, *Midnite Vultures* continues to sell well, however, and its tour has been a success.

Most of all, for Beck, it's been a success because for the first time fans are actually glad to have an acoustic interlude. For several years, going out on stage in a set where the band were either rocking up the proverbial storm or making the joint proverbially funky, where they were yelling for 'Loser' and 'Where It's At' and 'Debra' and demanding that the DJ entertain them, Beck found that the crowd were decidedly less enthusiastic when it came to the acoustic section of the show. (Possibly a decade of terrible MTV *Unplugged* specials, where old men try and make their songs look sexy by stripping them like chickens, has made the world resistant to hopeful-faced youths with acoustic guitars). But now, with an album of funk, the audience find themselves sufficiently sated with dance and have also had enough time to get nostalgic for the more wobbly, countrified moments of *Mutations*.

An acoustic interlude is also a lot safer. Playing in London, and leaping around during a funkier moment, Beck managed to get himself stabbed with a guitar, injuring himself quite badly (and, as the shocked press reported, miss his own aftershow party). Beck played down reports of his agonizing death. He seems to find the whole thing absurd, as though he had never read a newspaper or a gossip column before. He also pointed out that he is always wounding himself by accident. This seems, scarily, to be true. On one tour, he managed to put a three-inch cut right down his forearm. He has managed to break a blood vessel in his other arm. He has pulled a back muscle, and has gashed both his knees. The man should clearly be going onstage in an inflatable Sumo wrestler outfit; either that or hiring a stunt double for the more dangerous aspects of live work. Beck protests that the incident would never have been newsworthy if the promoter had not run out and immediately phoned the wire services. Yeah, right.

The point of this story, however, is not Beck's tendency to accidental self-harm, but rather his insistence that the whole affair – which was a bit more serious than a cut arm or a gashed knee – is somehow completely unimportant and in some vague way part of the absurd cult of celebrity that mars modern music. Even in a silly new story about an onstage injury, Beck won't be categorized. Beck Hansen, self-made man, non-ironic folk/hip hop/pop star, self-educated genius and anti-spokesman for a generation, still isn't willing to conform to anybody's idea of who he is, what he does, and how much pain he is in. He isn't part of anybody's mainstream. Kenny's Revenge will never end.

TWO

# THE MUSIC

## ALBUMS

Beck is one of the most prolific and eclectic albums artists of the past ten years. Where most acts are happy to release identical album after identical album, Beck never makes anything like the same record twice. And where other artists are happy to trickle out an album once every three or even four years, Beck has sometimes released four albums in a year. Lately, admittedly, this gush has reduced itself somewhat, as Beck finds himself touring and recording for a major label, but who knows what the future will bring? Lots of albums, with luck. The world also awaits with interest Beck's return to making the odd 'uncommercial' album, if not another *Stereopathetic Soul Manure*, then a second *Mutations*.

### Golden Feelings

Sonic Enemy, 1993 (cassette only)

US: did not chart

UK: did not chart

The Fucked Up Blues/Special People/Magic Stationwagon/No Money No Honey/Trouble All My Days/Bad Energy/Schmoozer/Heartland Feeling/ Super Golden Black Sunchild/Soul Sucked Dry/ Feelings/Gettin Home/Will I Be Ignored By The Lord?/Bogus Soul/Totally Confused/Muthafukka/ People Gettin Busy

*The first release by Beck to be available commercially and officially on a wide scale (previous cassette releases* Banjo Story *and* Fresh Meat And Old Slabs *did not enjoy a wide public, to say the least. In fact, it's safe to say that any copy you see purporting to be one or other of them is almost certainly a bootleg.) This cassette-only release came out on the Sonic Enemy label, which ceased to exist in 1995, and then returned from the dead quite recently.* Golden Feelings *was not, however, reissued by Sonic Enemy, on whose website is a message which under the heading 'WHERE'S BECK?' states, a little tersely, 'Beck doesn't live here anymore. Mommy says the mean lawyer people took him away to live with his other family, even though he lived with us first. Mommy says I'll understand someday.' Clearly the much-vaunted freedom to release uncommercial music that Beck had with Geffen doesn't seem to relate to* Golden Feelings, *whose raw quality may have finally decided Beck (or his lawyers) to stop the release coming out again (or maybe there are plans to release it through Geffen. Or perhaps it's going to be a ballet.) This is a shame: whatever the musical quality of the material here, which comes very definitely from that period in*

*Beck's career when he was mixing novelty songs with blues songs and the odd saunter into the macabre,* Golden Feelings *is a valuable document of the early part of Beck's career, before he met Carl Stephenson or became the darling of nations or was even within a mile of the faintest sniff of a hit record.*

*Essentially,* Golden Feelings *is an excellent opportunity for anyone who comes across a copy – naturally, there are bootlegs – to hear the sound of Beck inventing himself. And with songs like 'The Fucked Up Blues' (sample lyric: 'Well, the beans have been baking upon the camel's hump/Like a voodoo curse in an old lady's purse/Confetti on my grave/I got the fucked up blues'), 'Schmoozer' and 'Will I Be Ignored By The Lord', there is a real sense of something worthwhile and exciting being born. For those who despair of ever hearing any of* Golden Feelings, *however, do not worry, as several songs, like 'No Money, No Honey' and 'Gettin Home' would resurface on later recordings in one form or another. Beck doesn't let his puppies die.*

## A Western Harvest Field by Moonlight

Fingerpaint, 1994 (10" vinyl only)
US: did not chart
UK: did not chart

Big Side: Totally Confused/Mayonnaise Salad/Gettin Home/Blackfire Choked Our Death/Feel Like A Piece of Shit (Mind Control)/She Is All (Gimme

Something To Eat)/ Beek Side: Pinefresh/Lampshade/ Feel Like A Piece Of Shit (Crossover Potential)/ Mango (Vader Rocks!)/Feel Like A Piece Of Shit (Cheetoes Time)/Styrofoam Chicken (Quality Time)

*This vinyl-only release, attractively pressed as a vintage rockabilly-sized 10", came out in a very short run of 3,000 at the time, each record rather charmingly accompanied by a finger-painting made either by Beck or one of his friends at the party for the record's release. Later pressings, understandably, don't come with the finger-paintings. There's only so much finger-painting a man can do. The record came out again in an edition of 2,000 in 1995, 1,000 in 1997, and 1,000 again in 1998.*

*It's not hard to see why this record is so rare – it's really annoying. In between reasonable Beck tunes like 'Totally Confused' and the vexingly truncated 'She Is All (Gimme Something To Eat)', there is far too much doodling, funny noise and general messing around. At least the novelty aspects of* Stereopathetic Soul Manure *were funny; on* A Western Harvest Field By Moonlight, *every single track sounds like the bonus tune on a CD. The three 'Feel Like A Piece Of Shit' tracks are at least two too many and Beck's favourite trick – speeding voices up and down – is used, on 'Blackfire Choked Our Death', to the detriment of the song.*

*It's also a very short record. Beck has made singles which last longer than this; in the circumstances, the brevity of this album ought to be a good thing, but even while listening to the stupid looped groove of 'Styrofoam*

*Chicken (Quality Time)', which one bets even Beck has never listened to twice (but it's OK for us to sit through, wanting to hit Beck with a brick), the listener feels slightly cheated; if Beck was going to record such a self-indulgent mess, he could at least have done it properly.*

*There is an old Jewish joke about two ladies complaining about a meal. 'The food was terrible,' says one. 'Yes, and the portions were so small!' says her friend. That's pretty much what this album is like; terrible, and not enough of it.*

## Stereopathetic Soul Manure

Gusto Productions/Flipside, 1994

US: did not chart
UK: did not chart

Pink Noise (Rock Me Amadeus)/Rowboat/Thunder Peel/Waitin For A Train/The Spirit Moves Me/ Crystal Clear (Beer)/No Money No Honey/8.6.82/ One Foot In The Grave/Aphid Manure Heist/Today Has Been A Fucked Up Day/Rollins Power Sauce/Puttin It Down/11.6.45/Cut 1/2 Blues/ Jagermeister Pie/Ozzy/Dead Wild Cat/Satan Gave Me A Taco/8.4.82/Tasergun/Modesto/Bonus Noise

*Most people wait until they're getting near the end of their careers to release albums of out-takes, demos and alternative versions. It's typical of Beck that he released this record in the first year of his recording career. There*

may be more anarchic, disjointed, unconnected albums out there, some with sillier titles, dafter tributes to Ozzy Osbourne and powerful Germanic drinks, and stranger ones still warning about the nature of Satan's trickery, but it would be hard to name one. Certainly no-one else has ever pulled off the feat of putting both a future recording choice for the greatest living country singer of all time on the same album as some speeded-up nonsense talking about weed whackers. More than anything else in Beck's catalogue, Stereopathetic Soul Manure is the most idiosyncratic, eclectic and just plain silly record of the lot. And it's also very good.

Beck's second album of 1994 and his most anarchic ever, Stereopathetic Soul Manure is a kind of alternative greatest hits from a universe that's not so much parallel as sideways-on. The songs on this album were recorded over a period of several years, from 1988 to 1993, and some of them aren't songs at all. There are spoken-word rambles, country and western tunes, bits of Steven Hanft films, punk rock, real-life homeless people singing, sound effects and even a song which would be covered later by country legend Johnny Cash. Released to mixed reviews, Stereopathetic Soul Manure did enable Beck to establish himself as Mister Not Always Pop, and earned him the respect of fans for being prepared to release a record that at times is brilliant, and at others just borderline insane ranting.

Beck described this album best himself. When talking about the track 'Modesto', with its apparent reference to everyday alienation, Beck said, 'Everyone is alienated to some degree. How can you not be nowadays? These days, everything is fractured and fragmented, and that's what my music is made up of.' He's not wrong. Not only is *Stereopathetic Soul Manure* one of the most fractured and fragmented albums of all time – sometimes it sounds like Captain Beefheart's *Trout Mask Replica* recreated by some hyperactive children who didn't get to hear it all the way through – but Beck's description of it wins hands down over some other summaries. The best review ever of this album, in terms of scariness, is the one printed by the *Washington Student Daily*, which told the world that 'most of the songs on *A Western Harvest Field By Moonlight* or *Stereopathetic Soul Manure* are 'unbound noise conjunctions released from any pop concerns that might constrain his full-bore sonic collages.'

The best unbound noise conjunction released from any pop concerns that might constrain Beck's full-bore sonic collages here is probably the insane 'Pink Noise (Rock Me Amadeus)', which is a hoarse hardcore punk song with slide guitar that turns into feedback. It's strangely rather nice and not a lot like the Falco song of the same name, which is a shame. Interestingly, it claims to have been recorded in 1996, two years after the album came out. While this is not possible, unless Beck has access to some sort of folk music technology that the rest of the world does not know about yet, it's worth pointing out that this strange fascination with moving dates around is an extremely common feature of Beck's music. On several of his songs, throughout his career, he fiddles about with both time and titles. There's 'Whiskeyclone, Hotel City '97' from 1994's *Mellow Gold*, which shows no other indication of *having come from the future, there's the track listings on the 'Loser' single, which claim that two of the b-sides, 'Alcohol' and 'Soul Suckin Jerk (Reject)', were recorded in '19666'. On this album, too, there are the spoken word tracks '8.6.82' and '8.4.82', which may or may not date back to 1982, and weirdest of all, the spoken track, '11.6.45', which claims to have been recorded in 1945. This is unlikely, but may explain why at times Beck is clearly acting as though he is the reincarnation of some long-dead blues singer. He is the reincarnation of some long-dead blues singer.*

*The spoken word tracks are quite entertaining, not least because they display an early interest in experimentation by Beck. Very few other artists have been able to make avant-garde tracks just by walking around with a little tape recorder making things up about their day and then – via the medium of the half-dead battery – creating sped-up rants. And the spoken tracks, with their weed-whacker references, tie in nicely with the album's best-named track, 'Aphid Manure Heist', which begins with the sound of a leaf-blower, a popular instrument at early Beck shows, and then gets sillier. This was a time when Beck's work in people's gardens was having an influence on his music.*

*And while this is not an album for fans of melody, it does contain one of Beck's sweetest songs, the lilting and lugubrious 'Rowboat'. With its fine melody and sensible use of pedal steel, 'Rowboat' is a song so catchy and deep-voiced that it was later covered by Johnny Cash, who may or may not be aware of the credit on 'Satan Gave Me A Taco' to backing vocals by 'Johnny*

Cashmachine'. Equally, it's unlikely that Beck could have even dreamt that one day Cash, a singer who began his career making rockabilly records for Sun at the time Elvis Presley was there and went on to become one of the most important country singers of all time, would pick one of Beck's songs for one of his own records. (Cash's version is excellent, his deep, cracked voice perfectly suiting the song's melody and sounding oddly affecting on its simple, almost nursery-rhyme lyric.)

As befits an album that would one day inspire Johnny Cash (although it's doubtful he ever heard 'Pink Noise' or 'Aphid Manure Heist', which is a shame), country music is one of the biggest influences on this album. As well as 'Rowboat', there's the slow and edgy 'The Spirit Moves Me' ('I don't think it's funny when you shave both of my arms,' warns Beck, perhaps unnecessarily), and 'Crystal Clear (Beer)', with a very Beck lyric – 'Plastic donut, cup of spam/There's no goodness in this land'. Most interesting of all is 'Total Soul Future (Eat It)', which is essentially a country tune but has a falsetto soul vocal and a funky lyric. Despite its ramshackle arrangement and cheap playing, 'Total Soul Future (Eat It)' is the super-distant ancestor of Midnite Vultures. Beck also likes to point out that he first came to falsetto singing because it's a common feature of bluegrass recordings. (Falsetto is also used to excellent effect on the ludicrous punky 'Thunder Peel', the first Beck song to mention tacos and one where Beck launches into a Mick Jagger-esque falsetto as though old Mick were getting murdered.)

There are three recurrent types of songs, or rather recordings, on Stereopathetic Soul Manure – the silly *but entertaining spoken-word tracks, the field recordings with Ken the hobo, and songs from actual Beck live shows. The spoken-word tracks are just Beck walking around talking nonsense to himself into a tape recorder in which the batteries are nearly dead, creating a speeded-up effect. The tracks recorded with Ken are fascinating, however. Ken was apparently a homeless person who lived by a highway exit near Beck's home. He had been a real country and western singer living in Bakersfield, California, and as a consequence had a repertoire of classic country songs, from Johnny Cash to early country genius Jimmie Rodgers, who was known as 'The Singing Brakeman' and brought yodelling into popular music. Ken appears on Rodgers' 'Waiting For A Train' and also on a remake of 'No Money No Honey' from* Golden Feelings, *which is interminable and could have been a lot shorter than two minutes. Sadly, Ken has since moved on from his former address, and one hopes that news of the popularity of his (genuinely excellent) singing has reached him, wherever he is.*

*The live – and in the case of 'Satan Gave Me A Taco', fake live – tracks display Beck's penchant for novelty songs, which he claims were necessary to keep audiences happy and even awake in his early days. From the merely daft ('Ozzy', a kind of tribute to Black Sabbath's singer) to the slightly daft ('One Foot In The Grave', which mentions Satan and does not appear on the Beck album of the same name), the best of these live songs is easily 'Satan Gave Me A Taco', which combines two Beck obsessions – Satan and tacos – in an excellent comedy blues lyric. Of all the songs here, its lyrical con-*

*tent, which is both humorous and doomy, is most similar to the songs which would make up* Mellow Gold, *Beck's first 'proper' album.*

*With all this variety, low recording quality and stomach-churning veering from novelty blues to experimental fun to serious country and back to silly punk,* Stereopathetic Soul Manure *was never going to be a big hit record. It is, however, a charming one that even people who came to Beck through the huge pink mainstream music of* Midnite Vultures *will appreciate. It does, however, end – as do so many Beck records – with 'four minutes of silence and bonus noise', which may make the listener go mental. On the other hand, if the listener has got this far, they may well be ready for four minutes of silence and bonus noise.*

## Mellow Gold

DGC/Bong Load Custom Records, 1994

UK: 41

US: 13

Loser/Pay No Mind (Snoozer)/Fuckin With My Head (Mountain Dew Rock)/Whiskeyclone, Hotel City 1997/Soul Suckin Jerk/Truckdrivin Neighbors Downstairs (Yellow Sweat)/Sweet Sunshine/Beercan/Steal My Body Home/Nitemare Hippy Girl/Mutherfuker/Blackhole/Bonus Noise

*This is not one of Beck's favourite albums, although most people are very fond of it and it certainly contains sev-*

*eral of Beck's most memorable songs. Beck claims that the problem with the album is that he toured too much with the songs and 'hated them all'. Later, he remarked that after hearing them again, he realized that in the end* Mellow Gold *as a record was a lot like him, in that it has a noveltyish side.*

*In retrospect, Beck's qualms are a lot to do with time and opportunity. He's said that* Mellow Gold *wasn't really very representative of all of the things he wanted to do. He calls it the result of 'a lot of spontaneous silliness, and that's what it's like when you're hanging out with friends and you're coming up with ideas and throwing it together.'*

*More – or less – specifically, Beck told* Rolling Stone*: 'The whole concept of* Mellow Gold *is that it's like a Satanic K-Tel record that's been found in a trash dumpster. A few people have molested it and slept with it and half-swallowed it before spitting it out. Someone played poker with it, someone tried to smoke it. Then the record was taken to Morocco and covered with hummus and tabouli. Then it was flown back to a convention of waterskiers, who skied on it and played frisbee with it. Then the record was put on a turntable and the original K-Tel album had reached a whole new level.'*

*Beck actually felt embarrassed by aspects of* Mellow Gold *because, he felt, it was badly recorded. In fact much of it was recorded in three- or four-hour shifts at Carl Stephenson's house before Stephenson's girlfriend came home. This explains the album's spontaneous qualities, and marks it out as one of the least over-produced records of the time. Had Stephenson's girlfriend not been about to turn up every night,* Mellow Gold *might have come out sounding like* Dark Side Of The Moon.

*To be fair, Beck has also said, philosophically, 'That's not so bad, it pretty much reflected where I was at the time.'*

*And it does. From the album's title, a tribute (rather than an ironic reference) to the easy-listening albums that Beck had been into as a teenager, to the disbelieving line in 'Pay No Mind' where Beck sings 'I got signed', from the real life vignettes 'Truckdrivin Neighbors' and 'Nitemare Hippy Girl', and, most importantly, the generation-defining mixture of hip hop and blues on 'Loser',* Mellow Gold *is Beck's real debut album.*

*It has all the elements of both Beck's past and his future. There is surrealism and humour in the lyrics (check out what seems to be every Beck fan's favourite line, 'Like a giant dildo crushing the sun', in 'Pay No Mind'). There are little snatches of dialogue in the speeded-up diary style of* Stereopathetic Soul Manure. *There are songs with swearing in them like 'Fuckin With My Head' and 'Mutherfuker'. There is also the hip hop/blues of 'Loser' and the rocky drone of 'Whiskeyclone, Hotel City 1997'. And, naturally,* Mellow Gold *ends with a hidden track of electronic howling and yelps like a shortwave radio in season.*

*Beck remembers some tracks more fondly than others. The truck-driving neighbours were real people who really did live downstairs from Beck in an apartment in Los Angeles. He described them as 'horribly violent, genuine rednecks from Georgia or Alabama, drugged up in every way possible. I think that they were homosexuals who wouldn't dare admit it.' The events in the song – the fighting, the weaponry – all actually happened. Beck doesn't see the song as an anthem of hate. 'It was almost a kind of homage to these white-trash guys, he said later. (The sampled trucker shouts recall very much the similar real-life album* Shut Up Little Man!, *the recorded adventures of genuine drunk psychos Raymond and Peter). Beck was a little more acerbic about the possibly imaginary subject of 'Nitemare Hippy Girl' ('She's a self-inflicted obsession'); 'She was a flower child who had lost her petals,' he explained, 'Someone must have found them, rolled them up and made a cigarette, and then smoked them.'*

*And then there's 'Loser', a song which continues to vex Beck even now. While it will live forever because of its utterly imaginative fusion of blues guitar, dance rhythms and a rap delivery which draws a direct line from folk and blues to hip hop, 'Loser' will also be seen by many as the anthem of an imaginary slacker generation. Its lyrics, intended by Beck as a comment on his abilities as a rapper, were seen as a satirical comment on the MTV generation, a generation that Beck had never been part of. More interestingly, 'Loser' became the record grunge fans liked to dance to, and Beck was seen as the accessible, cleaner Kurt Cobain (Sub Pop, home of Nirvana, even put out a 'Loser' T-shirt as if to strengthen the connection.) Courtney Love has said that Cobain would have liked Beck if they had met, and Beck has said that when he heard Nirvana performing the old blues 'Where Did You Sleep Last Night', he realized that the* time was now right for his music. 'Loser' was thus really part of its era, in a way media commentators failed to notice.

'Loser' also opens Mellow Gold, as if to get it out of the way (a trick Beck also used in his live shows). In the end, while some of Mellow Gold is heavy going (for example, the dragging 'Sweet Sunshine'), it also contains much of Beck's best material. At worst, it created the template for the record that, most of all, defines Beck and made him one of the most original creative forces of the 1990s and beyond.

In the end, however, now that some time has passed since Mellow Gold's release, it can be seen as a lot more than just 'the album with "Loser" on it'. Mellow Gold sees Beck leaping instantly-formed as an artist who mixes seemingly opposing musical traditions and a pop style with a sound that had never previously existed. This is an extraordinary feat for a man who, barely a year before, was perceived as a novelty busker with a penchant for old folk and blues tunes.

Mellow Gold may well be seen by Beck as a serious record spoiled by novelty songs; but he's wrong. Mellow Gold introduces a completely new sound to pop music, for a start. It sets out Beck's stall as an artist, a man who does blend styles but is also not afraid to write straightforward country tunes or minimalist punk songs. It is a record with comedy lyrics on it, but there are hardly any, and what novelty numbers there are get a deadpan delivery which doesn't make them stand out like, say, the most annoying moments on a Beastie Boys record. For an album made by a man who had never really *worked with a producer before,* Mellow Gold *is astonishingly focused, complex and self-assured.*

*NB:* Mellow Gold *was released on vinyl in the US by Bong Load Custom. There are two important variants on the standard release of* Mellow Gold. *The first is the Australian version, which came with a 'tour sampler' CD which generously, if confusingly, was made up of tracks featuring 'Totally Confused' and 'Jagermeister Pie' from* Stereopathetic Soul Manure, *and 'Lampshade' and 'Rowboat' from* A Western Harvest Field By Moonlight. *The second is an American in-store promo version which, so as not to distress shoppers who have never been exposed to the tide of filth that is Beck's vocabulary, removes all the tracks with bad language in and replaces them with the popular rarity 'Corvette Bummer', itself one of the b-sides of 'Loser'.*

## One Foot In The Grave

K Records, 1994

US: did not chart
UK: did not chart

He's A Mighty Good Leader/Sleeping Bag/I Get Lonesome/Burnt Orange Peel/Cyanide Breath Mint/See Water/Ziplock Bag/Hollow Log/Forcefield/Fourteen Rivers, Fourteen Floods/Asshole/I've Seen The Land Beyond/Outcome/Girl Dreams/Painted Eyelids/Atmospheric Conditions

*In a year already flooded with Beck product, it was only*

natural that Beck should go up to Olympia, Washington State, and make yet another LP with his old friend Calvin Johnson from the group Beat Happening, down in Johnson's basement studio. Where Mellow Gold was recorded above ground, in lounges and living rooms, and features modern dance grooves and samples, this album was made in a dark basement in a cold northern town, and boy, does it show. This is a record where you can hear the hot mugs of coffee and the cold fingers stiffened by a brisk walk to the store to buy more panelled clothing.

An astonishingly assured and powerful record that would have made Beck the king of cult figures if he hadn't gone and spoiled it and recorded 'Loser', One Foot In The Grave is highly regarded by Beck fans as being his rootsiest album, and it is an impressive, simply recorded affair with a good floating band. Anybody interested in the side of Beck where there is no hip hop or dance music will derive serious pleasure from this album, which is in many ways the musical antithesis of Midnite Vultures. Where one is full of the colourful, glitter-ball spirit of living, loving black musicians, the other is a wintry echo of old people talking about death and the realities of life (all right, there are some novelty songs as well, and it's doubtful that Mississippi John Hurt ever wrote a tune called 'Cyanide Breath Mint'.)

This album pays tribute to Beck's musical heroes. He performs not one but two Mississippi John Hurt songs, 'He's A Mighty Good Leader' and 'Fourteen Rivers, Fourteen Floods'. On 'He's A Mighty Good Leader', Beck manages a ramshackle and strangely distanced-sound-

*ing vocal. This blues and folk style is a big part of his singing voice, and part of the appeal is his slight inability to sound like a sixty-five-year-old black man (on 'Fourteen Rivers, Fourteen Floods', a song helped along by some nice bottleneck guitar, Beck sounds as though he is singing with cotton wool in his cheeks). Nevertheless, Beck's versions of these songs have a dignity and lack of frivolity which is entirely successful. The same applies to 'I've Seen The Land Beyond', another Hurt song (not that you'd know it as* One Foot In The Grave *shares with* Stereopathetic Soul Manure *a reluctance to give songwriting credits. While no doubt all royalties were paid, Beck's stated love of his influences does not seem to extend to crediting them on his record sleeves).*

*Only Beck could follow a song like 'Fourteen Rivers, Fourteen Floods' by his idol Hurt with a song called 'Asshole'. 'Asshole' is a tribute to Pussy Galore, who were endemically fond of writing songs with rude titles. Despite its name, 'Asshole' is a brilliant song, fully formed and with an excellent lyric. At just two minutes long, it still sounds like an epic, and would be a must for an discerning Beck greatest moments compilation. A similarly fine song is 'Sleeping' which, with its droning groove and crooned melody, is easily good enough to be on* Mutations.

*There are clunky filler songs on* One Foot In The Grave, *like 'Girl Dreams', which goes nowhere slowly, and the mutated country of 'Painted Eyelids', but generally standards are high. The duets with Calvin Johnson are particularly effective. 'I Get Lonesome' is the best of* these, as Johnson's deep voice complements Beck's woozy tenor and the lyric – 'Getting fat on your own fear/ bring that beer over here' – marks 'I Get Lonesome' as a good song with a lyric that's actually about something for a change. 'Atmospheric Conditions' is the strangest, as Johnson leads Hansen through a draggy country punk duet which sounds like Merle Haggard's idea of a Brian Eno song.

The obligatory, in this era, songs with mad three-word titles on this occasion are 'Burnt Orange Peel', notable for a punk riff and for the wise use of Beck's falsetto, and the one-minute-thirty-five-seconds of 'Cyanide Breath Mint', a title Beck liked enough to name his publishing company after. The lyrics, about blood on the futon and a kid drinking fire, echo the words of 'Fucked-Up Blues' – 'I woke up on the futon and my boots were on fire'. Meanwhile 'Ziplock Bag' is the kind of song that would definitely not come out on Geffen, as a distorted guitar introduces distorted harmonica and distorted vocals, and 'Forcefield' is very atypical Beck, sounding almost like post-punk northern English bands The Fall or Joy Division, with Beck and vocalist Sam Jayne counterpointing each other's vocals as they sing two tunes at the same time.

At the time, One Foot In The Grave was seen as the flipside to Beck's dancier, more commercial and modernistic work. Now, as the likes of Mutations comes out on Geffen and Midnite Vultures offers a brassy, upfront version of Beck's dark side, the boundaries are a lot more blurred, and One Foot In The Grave sounds like it was made sixteen years before Midnite Vultures, *rather than just six, its primitive, bluesy ambience making it like the first* Rolling Stones *album compared to their recent stadium-pleasing epics. One Foot In The Grave comes from another world in more than one way.*

*NB: In Japan, where people are clearly hungrier for Beck than anywhere else in the world,* One Foot In The Grave *includes the three tracks from the 'It's All In Your Mind' single – 'It's All In Your Mind', 'Feather In Your Cap' and 'Whiskey Can Can'.*

## Odelay

---

DGC/Bong Load Custom Records, 1996

UK: 18

US: 16

Devil's Haircut/Hotwax/Lord Only Knows/The New Pollution/Derelict/Novacane/Jack-Ass/Where It's At/Minus/Sissyneck/Readymade/High 5 (Rock The Catskills)/Ramshackle/Bonus Noise

*'I have an idea for a section for* Odelay,*' joked Beck when this album came out, 'Hindu Trucker Goth Samba'.* Odelay *is such a varied, mad, eclectic album, full of psychedelia, country, spooky rock and exotic rhythms that Beck may actually have a point.* Odelay *is one of the great rock or pop or Hindu Trucker Goth Samba albums. The album that consolidated the promise of 'Loser',* Odelay *is more consistent, better produced and somehow more confident than* Mellow Gold. *It has better singles, sounds more exciting and, if every artist has one*

*album that we should all own, then* Odelay *is the Beck album for us all. Even his singing is better (a genuine Beck concern when he went into the studio to make this record). It's the* Purple Rain *or* Born In The USA *of Beck's career, an enormous cross-over record like* Nevermind *or* Thriller *that didn't change people's perceptions of Beck, but brought him into a wider arena. This was clearly an album by the man who had made 'Loser' a couple of years back, but one that broadened Beck's vision and made it more colourful and 3D, without sacrificing any of the ideas and ideals that had made Beck such a vital artist in the first place.*

*Critically,* Odelay *was liked by everybody in the world. Even Mike D from The Beastie Boys, another beneficiary of The Dust Brothers' production style, took time off from being a dickweed to say of Beck that 'he fits into the nomadic folk tradition of Ramblin' Jack Elliott, the whole traditional coffee house balladeer tip, but his hip hop side legitimizes Public Enemy as the real folk music of the '80s and '90s'. (Thanks, Mike, but did Public Enemy really need legitimizing as anything?)*

Odelay, *with its superb use of sampling and its seamless blend of folk, hip hop and 1960s rock, brought Beck's talent for making new sounds from old to the fore. Beck dislikes the idea that his sampled, mixed-up records are just examples of 'recycling', as he feels it cheapens the aesthetic and makes the music sound second class. For Beck, the way he makes music has 'a gracefulness and a dignity to it'. He describes his music as 'orchestrated, an organization of disparate elements'. Words like orchestrated and graceful are traditionally associated with the kind of work that Beck's father David Campbell does, tastefully putting strings and style on folk-rock records and making fairly sweet music sound even more sweet, but here Beck is paying tribute to the intricacy of his work, the way he takes elements that need not necessarily fit together – bits of 1960s rock, soundtrack voices, humour, rock and rap – and makes, not clunky, ill-fitting, look-ma-I'm-sampling records, but genuinely exciting and novel pop records. And certainly, on* Odelay*, this process came to such a peak, such a fantastic mixture of stylistic confidence, that it may explain why he decided to move away from it for* Midnite Vultures*, a record he describes as the 'official' follow-up to* Odelay*.*

*Beck conducted extensive interviews around the time of* Odelay*'s release. He talked about making a record that was very rhythmic and satisfying, that would have an interesting guitar sound and 'something completely different with the lyrics'. He was also starting to sound more comfortable in the studio. Once, his records had sounded raw and live; now they were the product of brilliant studio work. 'You have bands who try to make a record that reflects how they sound live, and I think what's the point?' he said, 'This is its own unique medium and I don't wanna have a record that sounds exactly like me playing live'.*

*There is not a bad track on* Odelay*, unless you count the traditional bonus noise at the end of the CD. Most tellingly of all,* Odelay *is one of those albums where everything sounds like a great single, and several tracks in fact are great singles. 'Where It's At' is a brilliant song,* one of the best singles Beck has ever released, and proof that folkies can dance. 'Devil's Haircut', with its Them (the Northern Irish 1960s R&B rockers led by one Van Morrison) sample – Odelay is more full of rock and guitar music than any other Beck album – is a thunderous opener. 'The New Pollution' is a groovy tune with an almost incomprehensible lyric, and 'Jack-Ass', as well as being a fine song, has the distinction of being the only Beck song available in a mariachi version (as 'Burro'), and is also, fact fans will be delighted to learn, the only Beck song beginning with 'J'. 'Sissyneck' offers a jauntier side of Beck and may well be the world's first country hip-hop record. 'Novacane' (are there any songs on this album that didn't come out as singles?) has a lovely, woozy bass, hip hop and harmonics at their most hypnotic with what sounds like the riff to The Osmonds' 'Crazy Horses' followed by part of 'Best Of My Love' by The Emotions. And of the songs that didn't come out as singles, 'Minus' is goth-punk, 'Ramshackle' is a dreamy and slightly spooky folk tune crying out for a cover version, 'Readymade' is typically trancey Beck but with a smart groove and 'Lord Only Knows' sounds like a (surreal) mission statement.

Odelay is possibly the best-realized of Beck's records (Midnite Vultures might also qualify for this title, but no-one apart from Beck seems to know exactly what it's meant to be). The Dust Brothers' production is superb, loud and (more unusually for Beck) clear throughout. Samples are used widely and wisely, and the record is the funkiest Beck had made to that date. It has a fantastically coherent sound (whereas Mellow Gold tend-

*ed to leap around a bit from style to style). And despite their well-known use of samples and general groove thang stuff, this is not a Dust Brothers album, but a Beck album. It's his use of melody, his unusual take on lyrics and his general attitude that dominates throughout.* Odelay, *for all its modern dance brilliance, is an album of songs, a collection of often brilliant melodies and, possibly, Beck represented at his best.*

*NB: As with* Mellow Gold, Odelay *was released on vinyl by Bong Load Custom. In Britain,* Odelay *has an extra track, the aptly-named 'Diskobox', which is a funky thing with distorted vocals. There is also, to make things more confusing, a limited edition UK version which has not only 'Diskobox' but also 'Clock', a song which turns up on the odd compilation as well. Australia, which issued a tour sampler CD with* Mellow Gold, *also has 'Diskobox', and another tour record, this time a 'tour' version of 'Sissyneck', along with 'Burro', the Dust Brothers remix of 'Dark And Lovely' and the previously unreleased 'Devil Got My Woman' and 'Brother'. Why does only Australia get all this stuff? What crimes has the rest of the world committed for Beck to withhold his bounty from us all?*

## Mutations

---

DGC/Bong Load Custom Records, 1998

UK: 14

US: 13

Cold Brains/Nobody's Fault But My Own/Lazy

Flies/Canceled Check/We Live Again/Tropicalia/ Dead Melodies/Bottle Of Blues/O Maria/Sing It Again/Static/Diamond Bollocks (unlisted)

*The cover, with Beck looking blank and wearing some polythene and the album's logo in futuristic lettering, suggests the contents are going to be some Bowie-esque future rock. Instead, despite the collaboration of Radiohead producer Nigel Godrich, who helped shape* OK Computer's *modernistic sound,* Mutations *is a record that in its own way is as rootsy as* One Foot In The Grave. *And as bleak: it's full of serious songs about grim themes, less of the silly humour and more of the dark imagery, or maybe, as the songs were all chosen by his girlfriend Leigh Limon (from Beck's precious songfilled notebook) just likes songs with titles like 'Dead Melodies', 'Cold Brains', 'Canceled Check' and 'Lazy Flies'. Even the jollier tunes like 'Bottle Of Blues' and 'O Maria' are obsessed with death.*

*But* Mutations *is not a glum record. It starts with the great 'Cold Brains', slow fuzzy guitar emphasizing the subtle rock production of Nigel Godrich, and then goes right into what may be Beck's most assured song yet, 'Nobody's Fault But Mine'. This track, with its Led Zeppelin title, sitar drone, and cello could equally be 1968-era 'head' rock or an Indian-esque out take from* Physical Graffiti. *Beck sings brilliantly with the dazed insomnia voice of John Lennon on 'I'm So Tired'. The phrase 'these wasted blues' is particularly effective. Despite the surrealist lyrics, this song more than any other shows how far Beck has moved from his novelty-songwriting days.*

*Another contender for a greatest hits compilation.*

*Everything else is also very good. 'Lazy Flies' is classic Beck in the form of a nonsensical and slightly creepy waltz. Fake harpsichord gives it a psychedelic, Hammer Horror film quality, and the guignol has never been grander. In similar mode, 'Canceled Check' is country with a typically twisted Beck melody. Gently rolling piano, steel guitar and some laid-back brass make this a very relaxed and human performance, capped by an excellent chorus. There is a brief yawning solo and the whole thing ends in what sounds like Gary Numan escaping his cage and trying to destroy the studio.*

*Cheerfulness abounds as a 'Girl From Ipanema' groove runs through the delightful and aptly-named 'Tropicalia', whose melody is vaguely derived from 1960s R&B singer Georgie Fame's 'Yeah Yeah'. Beck sounds like he is actually making cocktails in a big straw hat during this tune. Geffen must have roared with relief as, from an album of spooky waltzes and blues-folk songs, Beck had given his label a proper chirpy single. Similarly uptempo but more countryfied (Jew's Harp, clanky acoustic) is 'Bottle Of Blues', in which Beck sings that he has a bottle of blues but doesn't sound like it. As he raves on about black balloons and putting a nickel in a graveyard machine, he sounds like he's having the time of his life, and probably is.*

*In contrast, there are a lot of oddly delicate songs here too. With its harpsichord riff, delicate melody and strings, 'We Live Again' resembles The Rolling Stones' 'As Time Goes By' as rearranged to be sung by drowsy galley slaves. 'Oh, I grow weary of the end', sings Beck before informing the listener that 'love is a plague'. 'Dead Melodies' is also a waltz, this time with a quiet Mellotron underpinning and one that doesn't seem to have a lot of singing on it.*

*After the delightfully grim and chirpy 'O Maria' and the weakish 'Sing It Again',* Mutations *ends with the space-rock groove of 'Static' which sounds pretty much how a collaboration between early Leonard Cohen and early Pink Floyd might. It's a satisfying conclusion to an album which even Geffen felt deserved a wider (paying) audience (although in the end* Mutations *was, perhaps not surprisingly given its lack of funky monkey singles, not a big seller)*

*At last Beck has found a way of translating the wobbly country-folk sound of his early work into something contemporary. His singing throughout is excellent, suggesting an unrushed quality quite at odds with the album's two-weeks-only recording schedule.* Mutations *is the record that takes the quirky, country, folky side of Beck seen previously on* One Foot In The Grave *and proves that it can work in a commercial context. With its crisp production, superb melodies and air of confidence,* Mutations *was never going to end up coming out on a small indie label; it was, and is, strong enough to survive in the big world. It's a record that proves its point so strongly, that on his next album, Beck's change of direction was so extreme, in fact, that it suggests he also felt he could move on more dramatically.*

*NB: The US vinyl version of* Mutations *includes a 7" with 'Runners Dial Zero', and 'Diamond Bollocks'.*

*'Runners Dial Zero', name taken from a studio receptionist's entry code, is a fantastic, eerie, slow tune with a scary rumble laid underneath it. Arguably it would have sat rather well on the album proper. The epic 'Diamond Bollocks' – whose title is British slang for diamond testicles – is an exciting and quite bizarre mixture of Beatles-style psychedelia, Hendrix-esque funk, 1960s TV themes and people knocking things over. It ends with a nice bit of Mellotron, eventually.*

*The UK CD proudly lists 'Diamond Bollocks' on the sleeve, perhaps believing that British people will buy any record with the word 'Bollocks' on it, as well as 'Runners Dial Zero', making* Mutations *a rather fuller and more interesting release than the US version.*

*Just to confuse the issue, in Germany* Mutations *also has tracks from the 'Tropicalia' single, Skip Spence's 'Halo Of Gold' and Beck's own 'Black Balloon' (black balloons also being referred to on 'Bottle Of Blues'), while Japan has 'Runners Dial Zero' and a new version of 'Electric Music And The Summer People' recorded at the same time as the rest of the album. The Australian version of* Mutations *lets itself down by having, not a tour EP or single, but a solitary bonus track, 'Runners Dial Zero'.*

**Right** Fresh-faced and clear-eyed, Beck's greatest bugbear is that the world thinks he is 12.

**Left** Andy Warhol, silver-wigged former employer of Beck's mother Bibbe Hansen.

**Above** Early Beck hero Woody Guthrie. Note prominent fascist-killing guitar warning label.

**Left** Beck, putting his acoustic roots to work.

**Left** Dressed by his girlfriend Leigh Limon, Beck cuts a stylish figure onstage and off. Generally.

**Right** Bob Dylan, icon to millions and a Beck influence, wearing a wicker basket on his head.

**Above** A charismatic live performer, Beck is part preacher…

**Left** … and part busker.

**Left** As non-Britpop as can be, Beck was one of the successes of the 1997 Glastonbury Festival.

**Right** Less successful was this limited edition moustache, later blown away in a light breeze.

**Above and left** With 1999's Midnite Vultures, Beck got the funk, while critics got the hump.

**Above** LA, down-to-earthness, humour and cool – these are the essential elements of Beck, past, present and future.

## Midnite Vultures

DGC, 1999

UK: 19

Sexx Laws/Nicotine & Gravy/Mixed Bizness/Get Real Paid/Hollywood Freaks/Peaches & Cream/ Broken Train/Milk & Honey/Beautiful Way/Pressure Zone/Debra

*Every great musician makes an album that no-one understands at the time. Admittedly, so do all the bad musicians, and many albums that no-one understands often turn out to be awful. However,* Midnite Vultures *is a strong contender for a truly great misunderstood album. Partly as a result of most rock critics not really liking or understanding dance music, and partly because people like their variety to be, well, not that varied,* Midnite Vultures *is the first Beck album to come in for any kind of confused criticism. It's also the first time that Beck has had to stop being self-deprecating about what he sees as the faults of his albums and start actually defending his work.*

*Around the time of* Odelay, *Beck was talking about a 'slow jam' he'd written called 'I Want To Get With You'. He said he'd become obsessed with slow, sexy R&B tunes 'because a lot of them are really LA. If you listen to a lot of lyrics, like R. Kelly's "I Like The Crotch On You", he's really talking about his sexuality at the time. And he's heartfelt. So the song that I wrote is really drawing from that world, because it's coming from me. I didn't* want it to be seen as a parody.'

A year or two later, 'I Want To Get With You' had become 'Debra', and the cornerstone of Beck's most controversial and imaginative album. With the templates of Odelay and Mutations, Beck had given himself a job for life, but, in time-honoured artistic fashion, he chucked the lot to make the bump 'n' grind disco inferno (in both senses of the word) album Midnite Vultures.

He told journalists just before this album came out that he was going to release a 'dumb-ass party record'. This may be the case, but Midnite Vultures isn't that album. Midnite Vultures is a fun, funny and exciting record, but also one full of what Beck describes as 'themes of decadence, debauchery, saturation, the cultural miasma'.

Musically, unless you want to hear 'Where It's At' until you die, Midnite Vultures is excellent, from 'Sexx Laws' with its great opening line 'Can't you hear those cavalry drums?' and its banjo outro, to the 1980s groove of 'Hollywood Freaks' with its speeded-up Funkadelic backing vocal, a grumbling bass and classic old school claptrap percussion and Eminem-type slurred rap and 'Debra', which, despite its funky perfection, is one of the oldest songs here, a 'Rainy Night In Georgia' intro and Ramsey Lewis sample behind a vocal very reminiscent of early Prince. 'Get Real Paid' has a fantastic chant and a great Kraftwerk riff.

But this record is not all funk. 'Beautiful Way' is a love song with a fairly straightforward, slightly Dylan-esque lyric, a dreamy arrangement and some harmonica that could easily fit on Mutations. And, despite its Tone-Loc *groove and spraycan-rattle sample, 'Pressure Zone' has a classic* Odelay *stomp and a* Mutations*-type lyric ('Masterpieces liquidate in fertile tears/I could sleep inside her bones/A hundred years'). In fact, while the first half of* Midnite Vultures *is Beck-type funk, the second half is much more Beck with slight funky trappings. There's the strange Bowie-esque chant on 'Peaches & Cream', the hard-rock grind and Lynyrd Skynyrd guitar on 'Milk & Honey' by ex-Smith Johnny Marr, the appearance of dance folkie Beth Orton on 'Pressure Zone'. And in general, the lyrics, while hardly Hallmark greeting card-basic, have a directness and clarity missing from earlier Beck. A lot of songs are in the first person.*

*Beck also remarked that he was trying to create 'Topanga moments', meaning the 'burned out-in-the-canyon vibe' achieved so easily by fucked-up LA rock stars in the 1970s. At its best,* Midnite Vultures *is social comment masquerading as an orgy. The opening robotic chant of 'Get Real Paid' just oozes emptiness, while 'Milk & Honey' claims, 'No it isn't funny/Living in a garden of sleaze'.*

*This album breaks all boundaries. It's not a funky party, it's the sound of Beck commenting on the coke and glam life of LA, the emptiness at the heart of wealth and casual sex, and doing so using its own soundtrack. On 'Broken Train', 'Billionaires smile like weapons/Passing out platinum pensions/They're out of control/No one knows how low they'll go', is hardly a line celebrating the champagne lifestyle (and musically, it most resembles the songs on* Odelay*, even throwing in a little snatch of the 'New Pollution' melody). Even the clearly sexed-up*

*'Peaches & Cream', which is also the most Prince-like track here (and whose title even combines those of two Prince songs), is not your average funk-sex number. Again, it's Stonesy – 'You make a garbage man scream' echoes the infamous 'You make a dead man come' on 'Start Me Up' and contains the very Beck-like line 'Give those pious soldiers/Another lollipop/Cause we're on the good ship Menage A Trois'.*

*Beck has been criticized for making* Midnite Vultures, *probably by people who thought he should just be making* Odelay *again until he bursts. (Some were worried by the apparent sexism of Beck's new lyrics, previously cuddly and droll if a little dark. They needn't be; he's having fun at everyone's expense, but mostly his own.) Beck, not working for other people, said, 'Where do you edit yourself? Where do you define boundaries about what you should and shouldn't do? Most of me tends to not want to care about doing the wrong thing.'*

*NB: The Japanese version of* Midnite Vultures *features the bonus track 'Arabian Nights', while a special US version found in Best Buy stores came with a CD featuring 'Salt In The Wound', 'This Is My Crew' and the Malibu Mix of 'Sexx Laws' by Roger Manning.*

## Stray Blues: A Collection of B-sides

Geffen (Japan), 2000

Totally Confused/Halo Of Gold/Burro/Brother/Lemonade/Electric Music And The Summer People/Clock/Feather In Your Cap

*Indeed this is a collection of B-sides, but it isn't a very comprehensive collection of B-sides, being just eight songs from an artist famous for prolific song production. Not a particularly imaginative or ergonomic use of the CD format. The world awaits* Stray Blues II *with breath that is far from bated.*

## SINGLES

Beck is one of the most exciting singles artists of recent years, partly because he releases great snappy pop tunes like no-one else's, and partly because he has helped to revive the art of the B-side, in that, where most rock artists now slap any old nonsense on a CD single, Beck would produce new, unusual unreleased material that had clearly never been intended for album release. Now, however, he seems quite happy to be Dance Beck and just release endless remixes. He's also extremely fond of reworking songs, ensuring that even if you have every single one of his songs, you may not have every single version. Later releases, people who don't like dance music should be warned, may have exciting, song-like titles but are generally remixes of A-sides. Thus Beck moves from shambolic, grinning folkie to robotic monster king of the disco-rave dancefloor, and the world, grateful, moves with him.

## MTV Makes Me Want To Smoke Crack (Beck) / To See That Woman Of Mine (Beck)/ Privates On Parade (Bean)/Rock-Scissors-Paper (Bean)

Gusto Productions/Flipside, 1993

*There are only a thousand copies of this 7" single, pressed on sexy blue vinyl. 'MTV Makes Me Want To Smoke Crack' is Beck in his acoustic humorist phase, with lyrics about everyone and everything on MTV being perky and nice. This being Beck's first-ever single, of course, it's unlikely he believed at the time that he would ever be on MTV. Nevertheless, this fine and accurate critique of the simpering oaf that is Music Television remains the best song ever written about MTV (certainly compared to Dire Straits' grim 'Money For Nothing'). Beck's portrayal of a happy, smiling dead world is a direct descendant of Talking Heads' 'Heaven' and suggested to the listener (well, suggested to the 1,000 listeners lucky enough to get a copy of 'MTV Makes Me Want To Smoke Crack') that a man of deep cynicism and powerful, cutting humour is about to launch himself on the world. 'To See That Woman Of Mine' is a nice acoustic number with a folky lyric and side two of the record is shared with local group Bean, members of whom have worked with Beck on later occasions. NB: 'MTV Makes Me Want To Smoke Crack' was later reprised, in a new version that went 'lounge' halfway through, for the benefit of British singles buyers who had wisely decided to listen to the B-side of 'Loser'.*

## Loser/ Steal My Body Home

Bong Load Custom Records, 1993

*The song that crystallized slackerdom, invented a new kind of music with no name, and made Beck a star around the world, 'Loser' is still a striking single today. From Carl Stephenson's hip hop beats to the Dr John sample from 'Walk On Gilded Splinters' and Beck's own slide guitar riff, 'Loser' is a brilliantly original piece of music constructed from a variety of seemingly conflicting sources. Beck's lyric takes the song into another world-weary yet hilarious dimension. Nothing was to be the same again, as even Beck was to find himself annoyingly defined as some kind of slacker king by the entire world (ironically as, given that James Brown is now quite old, Beck must actually be the hardest-working man in showbusiness). A whole generation was conjured up overnight, and this song became their anthem (although research suggests that there actually were no slackers, except for Beavis and Butthead, who were cartoon characters and therefore don't count).*

*By contrast, the hip hop-less 'Steal My Body Home' turns up again on* Mellow Gold, *where its slow, lugubrious nature is happy and at home.*

## Loser/Corvette Bummer/Alcohol/Soul Suckin' Jerk (Reject)/ Fume

DGC/Bong Load Custom Records, 1994

*Fame comes to Beck as Geffen pick up on 'Loser', chuck*

*on a plethora of unreleased tracks and launch Beck into a willing world (and the DGC/Bong Load link-up ensured that this was, and still is, the most successful independent single in the history of recorded music, which is not bad for a record made in someone's front room). The extra tracks are all very good – 'Corvette Bummer' with its bluesy opening line 'All my days I had moldy bread' and reference to a ziplock bag (one of Beck's many favourite things, in song, is a ziplock bag), is a cool rap with a great bassline, 'Alcohol' is a dreamy acoustic thing which perfectly sums up what it's like to drink, and possibly even be, some alcohol. 'Soul Suckin Jerk (Reject)' is, as its title suggests, a different, rougher version of the* Mellow Gold *track, and 'Fume' is just rocking, in the* Stereopathetic Soul Manure *tradition.*

*Fans of Beck's cavalier and perhaps sarcastic approach to liner notes were delighted to see that, in classic Beck time-travel fashion, the sleeve claims that 'Loser' was recorded in 1982, 'Fume' in 1988 and all other tracks in '19666'. It was a very good year, 19666.*

## Loser/MTV Makes Me Want To Smoke Crack/Corvette Bummer/Totally Confused

Geffen/Bong Load Custom Records, 1994

*Another rejig, this time including the soon-to-be-everywhere new version of 'Totally Confused', originally on* A Western Harvest Field By Moonlight*.*

## Loser/Alcohol/Fume

Geffen/Bong Load Custom Records, 1994

*A UK 7" limited edition of 1,500 copies. (For many years after this, Beck singles would for some reason always come out in the UK in a special 7" limited edition of 1,500 copies. No-one knows why.)*

## Loser/Alcohol

DGC/Bong Load Custom Records, 1994

*A jukebox 45, one of the last ever, possibly, and very handy for people who lived in swamps or Arctic tracking stations and wanted to hear the new slacker craze satirized as they wondered if* The A-Team *had been cancelled.*

## Steve Threw Up/Mutherfuker/Untitled

Format: 7" (BL 11)

Bong Load Custom Records, 1994

*This 7" single is an always-popular item in any Beck fan's catalogue. The 'Steve' of the track is Steve Moramarco from Bean, who shared the flipside of the 'MTV Makes Me Want To Smoke Crack' single, and the song details his unfortunate vomiting problems after riding on a Ferris wheel. Its lyrical highpoint, in fact, is a list – a veritable itinerary – of the things that Steve had eaten and then brought forward from his stomach. The moral of the story is, if you want Beck to write a song about you, throw up in front of him. Oddly, Geffen did not beg to release this one. 'Motherfuker' and 'Untitled' are similarly anarchic affairs. A big Beck trio of fun.*

## Beercan/Got No Mind/Asskizz Powergrudge (Payback '94)/ Totally Confused/Spanking Room /Loser (Unlisted)

DGC/Bong Load Custom Records, 1994

*Weird playing-with-head version activity here. 'Beercan' is a delightful tune known to fans of* Mellow Gold, *while 'Got No Mind' is a different version of 'Pay No Mind' from the same album, and 'Loser' appears in a very strange version. 'Spanking Room' and 'Asskizz Powergrudge (Payback '94)' display differing forms of powerful noise and, oh look, it's 'Totally Confused' again. How many songs can you get on one single? In the olden days, they would have called this a mini-album.*

## It's All In Your Mind/ Feather In Your Cap/Whiskey Can Can

K Records, 1995

*This 7" contains material not released from the sessions Beck did with Calvin Johnson in 1993. As a consequence, it doesn't sound much like the material the big world was getting used to from Beck. But then, that was the whole idea. An acoustic number with a basic chorus, as is prevalent on the Johnson sessions, 'Whiskey Can Can' is a chirpy tune to say the least, which returns to one of Beck's favourite themes (generally, booze, and specifically, whiskey) while 'Feather In Your Cap' is a song we shall meet again, as Beck likes it a lot. Some of these singles are pressed in see-through brown vinyl, just to make life even more difficult for obsessive record collectors who have to have the same record twice just because it's a different colour.*

## Pay No Mind (Snoozer)/Special People/Trouble All My Days/Supergolden (Sunchild)

Geffen/Bong Load Custom Records, 1994

*Possibly to divert interest away from the Sonic Enemy release of* Golden Feelings, *or just to make tracks available to the poor folk of the wintry isles, this (swiftly withdrawn) UK single features three songs from Beck's first proper release. They contrast rather nicely in their bluesiness, acoustic simplicity and oddness – there is yodelling on 'Supergolden (Sunchild)'– with the dour power of 'Pay No Mind', whose bracketed title, 'Snoozer', is a tribute not to its dullness (it's not dull at all) but to its fantastically hypnotic droning quality.*

## Pay No Mind/Special People

Geffen/Bong Load Custom Records, 1994

*1,500-only 7" single in Britain. Very nice. And they say* A Western Harvest Field By Moonlight *is rare.*

## Where It's At (Edit)/Where It's At (Mario C. And Mickey P. Remix)/Bonus Beats

Geffen/Bong Load Custom Records, 1996

*The classic 'two turntables and a microphone' single, a record which showed that Beck could be a powerful commercial force as well as an imaginative one. Here, 'Where It's At' (a title that just makes the listener want to add 'Two turntables and a microphone') is wisely coupled with a remix and some bonus beats. This is Australia's version.*

## Where It's At (Edit)/Where It's At (Mario C. And Mickey P. Remix)/Bonus Beats/Where It's At (Remix By U.N.K.L.E.)

Geffen/Bong Load Custom Records, 1996

*This EP is the British version of the Australian single listed above.*

## Where It's At (Edit)/Make Out City (Remix By Mike Simpson)/Where It's At (Remix By Mario C. And Mickey P. )/Where It's At (Remix By John King)/ Bonus Beats (Previously Unreleased)

DGC/Bong Load Custom Records, 1996

*The American version of the two singles listed above.*

### Where It's At (Edit)/Where It's At (Remix By John King)/ Lloyd Price Express (Remix By John King)/Dark And Lovely (Remix By Dust Brothers)/American Wasteland (Remix By Mickey P.)/Clock

The Japanese version of the three singles listed above. All these titles, by the way, refer to remixes of 'Where It's At', except for 'Clock', which is an interesting song that turns up, like all Beck's interesting songs, in quite a few different places.

### Devils Haircut (LP Version)/Dark And Lovely (Remix By Dust Brothers)/American Wasteland (Remix By Mickey P.)/000.000

Geffen/Bong Load Custom Records, 1996

*Beck's crunchiest single, thanks to the sampled 'I Can Only Give You Everything' riff, accompanied by a brilliantly woozy vocal and a lyric inspired by, what else, the blues filtered through Beck's personal viewpoint. UK and US versions are the same, but in the UK one gets '000.000' which is, essentially, strange noise.*

### Devils Haircut (Remix By Noel Gallagher)/Groovy Sunday (Remix By Mike Simpson)/Trouble All My Days

Geffen/Bong Load Custom Records, 1996

*This is part two of the UK single. Oasis' main man remixes 'Devil's Haircut' in a way that apparently divided fans at the time (ie, half of them hated it) and 'Trouble All My Days' turns up again.*

## The New Pollution/The New Pollution (Remix By Mario C. & Mickey P.)/Lemonade

Geffen/Bong Load Custom Records, 1997

*The British version of another fine, chunky single from* Odelay, *the third from an album quite capable of firing out singles like a spawning musical salmon. 'Lemonade' features Spinanes vocalist Rebecca Gates and is quite mad.*

## The New Pollution/Richard's Hairpiece (Remix By The Aphex Twin)/Electric Music And The Summer People

Geffen/Bong Load Custom Records, 1997

*Another version of the single, this time with a new version of 'Electric Music And The Summer People', which was originally a very different song scheduled for, but left off,* Odelay, *an album which seems to have changed itself all the time as things progressed. Beck is nothing if not a very organic recording artist.*

### The New Pollution And Other Favorites EP: The New Pollution/The New Pollution (Remix By Mickey P.)/The New Pollution (Remix By Mario C. And Mickey P.)/Richard's Hairpiece (Remix By The Aphex Twin)/Thunderpeel/Lemonade/000.000/Feather In Your Cap

Geffen/Bong Load Custom Records, 1997

*Japan goes rarity crazy, with mixes and unreleased tracks galore. Two of the songs here made obsessive fans sigh with relief as at first glance they are oldies but, alas, no. 'Thunderpeel' is a different version of the* Stereopathetic Soul Manure *song, while the new version of 'Feather In Your Cap' is from the* Suburbia *soundtrack. He's a busy man, Beck.*

### The New Pollution (LP Version)/The New Pollution (Remix By Mickey P.)

Geffen/Bong Load Custom Records, 1997

*Otherwise dull and unimaginative European coupling of tracks, made to look sexier with CD-ROM video-clips of 'Where It's At' and 'The New Pollution'.*

### Sissyneck/The New Pollution (Remix By Mickey P.)/Feather In Your Cap (From Suburbia Soundtrack)

Geffen/Bong Load Custom Records, 1997

Odelay's *fourth and daftest single, and some tracks*

*someone, somewhere might not have, for the UK market. This singles also came out in Britain as – what else? – a limited edition 1,500 copy 7".*

### Sissyneck/Burro/Dark And Lovely (Remix By Dust Brothers)/Devil Got My Woman/Brother

Geffen/Bong Load Custom Records, 1997

*Much more fun, this Australian tour edition contains a couple of very fine songs in (Skip James') 'Devil Got My Woman' and Beck's own 'Brother' and has the great mariachi version of 'Jack-Ass'. Beck should tour Australia more often, it's clearly very good for his B-sides.*

### Jack-Ass (Butch Vig Mix)/Jack-Ass (Lowrider Mix By Butch Vig)/Burro/Strange Invitation/Devil Got My Woman/Brother

Geffen/Bong Load Custom Records, 1997

*A single with some old friends and 'Strange Invitation', a lovely orchestral version of 'Jack-Ass', conducted by Beck's dad, David Campbell. All these tracks came out, amazingly, as a 7" single, which must have been the musical equivalent of putting a bloody great ship in a tiny bottle.*

### Deadweight (Edit)/Erase The Sun/SA-5

Geffen, 1997

*'Deadweight' is a Latin-styled song specially written for the movie* A Life Less Ordinary. *'Erase The Sun' is a loud acoustic song with lines reused on 'Diamond Bollocks', while 'SA-5' is the same sort of thing, only without recyclable lyrics.*

## Tropicalia/Halo Of Gold/Black Balloon

Geffen/Bong Load Custom Records,1998

*More Latin pop, this is the first 45 from* Mutations *and features 'Halo Of Gold', the Skip Spence tune, and the cheery 'Black Balloon'. Came out in Britain, astonishingly, as a 7" single in a limited edition of 1,500. Are there just 1,500 Beck fans in Britain who don't have CD players?*

## Cold Brains/Electric Music And The Summer People/Halo Of Gold/Runners Dial Zero/Diamond Bollocks

Geffen/Bong Load Custom Records, 1999

*A nice promo single, wisely eschewing a lot of famous hit singles for a delightful album track and some particularly fine strangeness.*

## Nobody's Fault But My Own/One Of These Days/Diamond In The Sleaze

Geffen/Bong Load Custom Records, 1999

*Japan got the lovely 'Nobody's Fault' and a few extra songs. 'One Of These Days' is a fine tune, as is 'Diamond In The Sleaze'. A hat-trick, then.*

## Sexx Laws/This Is My Crew/Sexx Laws (Wiseguys Remix)

Geffen, 1999

*The funk kicks in, with one of the many fine songs off the underrated* Midnite Vultures. *'Sexx Laws' has a great riff, a hilarious and acerbic lyric and a great new change of direction that must have pissed off a few million folkies. DJ Swamp scratches with aplomb on 'This Is My Crew'. Amongst the versions, this time a 7" picture disc.*

## Mixed Bizness/Mixed Bizness (Nu Wave Dreamix By Les Rythmes Digitales)/Dirty Dirty

Geffen, 2000

## Mixed Bizness/Mixed Bizness (Cornelius Remix)/Mixed Bizness (DJ Me DJ You Remix)/Mixed Bizness (Video)

Geffen, 2000

*Another good* Midnite Vultures *song, this time accompanied by a whole world of mixes and the aptly-named new song 'Dirty Dirty'. Beck appears on an LP by Cornelius' girlfriend, you know.*

### Mixed Bizness (Nu Wave Dreamix By Les Rythmes Digitales)/Mixed Bizness (Cornelius Remix)/Mixed Bizness (DJ Me DJ You Remix)/Dirty Dirty/Saxx Laws (Night Flight To Ojai)

Geffen, 2000

*More mixes. Well, it is a dance record. There's also a German single of 'Mixed Bizness' with a Transatlantik mix called 'Die Fantastischen Vier' and a European single with a new track, 'Arabian Nights'. The times being what they are in the world of Beck, 'Arabian Nights' is not a wobbly acoustic tune recorded in a basement, but an uptempo funking groover.*

## COMPILATIONS

As befits an artist who favours eclecticism, live work and proliferation, Beck appears on possibly more compilations than any other person in the 1990s. Much of the material on these collections is available elsewhere, albeit on rare 45s, while Beck's fondness for live material ensures that there are plenty of alternative versions of songs. Only a billionaire or a lunatic would buy all these records, mind, so if you are a big fan, try and find yourself a billionaire or a lunatic, or both.

## Various Artists
## Rare On Air: Live Performances Volume 1

Mammoth, 1994

*A compilation from an LA radio station's live sessions, this album ranges across the whole spectrum of Los Angeles' finest music, from Lindsey Buckingham of Fleetwood Mac to X, and also takes in some other troubadour types – Nick Cave, Tori Amos, Leonard Cohen. The ur-Beck, Evan Dando, appears, while Beck himself is represented by a live version of 'Mexico', from* A Western Harvest Field By Moonlight. *A consistent collection, where Beck doesn't stick out like a sore folkie.*

## The Geraldine Fibbers
## Get Thee Gone

Sympathy For The Record Industry, 1994

*Friends of Beck, The Geraldine Fibbers invite him (and Chris Ballew from The Presidents Of The United States Of America) to appear on 'Blue Cross', a song co-written by Beck. This record came out, as records associated with Beck often do, on 10" vinyl, and was reissued later on with extra tracks.*

## Various Artists
## KXLU 88.9 FM, Los Angeles Live Vol. I

KXLU, 1995

*Another radio station compilation. Beck offers up the marvellously-named 'Whiskey-Faced, Radioactive, Blowdryin Lady', a song which is about as self-explanatory as it gets. (Note constant refusal by Beck to use apostrophes.)*

## Jon Spencer Blues Explosion
## Orange

Matador, 1994

*Former Pussy Galore man (and thus hero to Beck) produces immense, noisy record and asks Beck to come in and rap on one track, the equally immense and noisy 'Flavor'.*

## Various Artists
## DGC Rarities Vol. I

DGC, 1994

*Continuing Beck's policy of appearing on every album released in 1994, here he appears with other artists from DGC's line-up that year, this time performing the extremely rare 'Bogus Flow'. Sympathetic Beck is here surrounded by songs from Weezer and Sonic Youth (with 'Compilation Blues').*

## Various Artists
## Swag

Geffen, 1994

*Beck contributes 'Loser' B-side 'Corvette Bummer' alongside tracks by Hole, Weezer, Sonic Youth and, er, Pat Metheny.*

## Jabberjaw
## Good to The Last Drop

Mammoth Records, 1994

*Artists associated with the club where Beck was discovered by Bong Load here contribute tracks to a Jabberjaw compilation. Beck supplies the suitably funk-related 'In A Cold Ass Fashion', which was recorded with Carl Stephenson.*

## Various Artists
## Jabberjaw

Mammoth Records, 1994

*This 1,500-only 7" is a rare example of the compilation single. Beck is joined by Hole, Jawbox and Scotland's lovely Teenage Fanclub.*

## Various Artists
## CMJ New Music Monthly

CMJn, 1994

*Free CD with the September issue of CMJ, featuring Beck's 'It's All In Your Mind'.*

## Various Artists
## Periscope: Another Yo Yo Compilation

Yo Yo, 1994

*Notable for some of America's best ever band names – Neutral Milk Hotel, Go Sailor, Excuse 17 and Bloodthirsty Butchers (with 'I Hate You Bucket'), this compilation also features Beck's uncommon The 'World May Loose Its Motion'.*

## Nardwuar The Human Serviette
## Skookum Chief Powered Teenage Zit Rock Angst Presented By Nardwuar The Human Serviette

Nardwuar the Human Serviette, 1995

*Nardwuar The Human Serviette is a Canadian comedy interviewer who phones people up and talks to them incoherently. He's not very funny, as his interview with half-Canadian Beck shows. This CD, which came with a free CD of 'Loser', features several Canadian acts and the Beck interview which memorably ends with Beck telling Nardwuar to 'fuck off'.*

## Jon Spencer Blues Explosion
## Experimental Remixes

Matador, 1995

*'Flavor again', this time remixed on an EP in two parts, by Beck, Mike D from the Beastie Boys, and Beck's DJ chum Mario Caldato Jr.*

## Various Artists
## Fast Forward #2

Brinkman, 1995

*A double CD of music from a Dutch festival. Beck performs 'Trouble All My Days', a song he lets loose about as often as he can.*

## Caspar And Mollüsk
## Caspar And Mollüsk

Cosmic Records, 1995

*Caspar is Chris Ballew from The Presidents Of The United States Of America and Mollüsk is Beck. No-one knows why. This yellow vinyl album was recorded on the cheap in bedrooms and on four-track machines. Beck appears on one track, 'Twig', later redone by The Presidents Of The United States Of America without him.*

**Various Artists**
**Un Hiver '95**

Geffen/Carrere, 1995

*Free with French rock magazine* Les Inrockuptibles, *this compilation features Beck's 'Beercan' and 'Mexico'.*

**Various Artists**
**The Poop Alley Tapes**

Win, 1996

*Beck contributes 'Girl Dream', originally on* One Foot In The Grave.

**Various Artists**
**Volume 16: Copulation Explosion**

Volume, 1996

*With a free CD-ROM, this compilation of new recordings by various indie bands from the US and the UK features a new version of Beck's 'Thunderpeel'.*

**Various Artists**
**Yo Yo A Go Go**

Yo Yo, 1996

*A collection of live material from the Yo Yo A Go Go festival in Olympia, Washington State. Beck performs 'Title Unknown' and 'Sleeping Bag'.*

## Various Artists
## Buy Product 2: Brief Encounters

DGC/Geffen/Almo, 1996

*Another sampler from Geffen. Beck contributes 'Novacane' and Sonic Youth bust a gut on an instrumental of 'Little Trouble Girl'.*

## Various Artists
## Vans Warped Music Sampler

Vans, 1996

*As Beck's official website points out, Beck appears on this compilation but wasn't on the accompanying tour. Life is easier like that. He is represented by 'Make-Out City (Where It's At Remix)', which suggests he was not exactly going to push the boat out on this one.*

## Various Artists
## Swagalicious

Geffen Records/DGC, 1996

*A promotional CD. Beck donates 'Clock'.*

**Various Artists**
**MuchMusic Presents: Big Shiny Tunes**

MuchMusic, 1996

*A Canadian label compilation, featuring major alternative bands like Garbage and Foo Fighters, pop from No Doubt and Fun Lovin' Criminals and, again, 'Novacane' from Beck.*

**Various Artists**
**Just Say Noel**

Geffen, 1996

*Beck, having failed to appear on any Christmas records so far, joined Sonic Youth ('Santa Doesn't Cop Out On Dope') and others for this festive effort, contributing the drolly-named and utterly aptly-titled 'Little Drum Machine Boy'. A generous gesture, for a man once so poor he used to dread Christmas.*

**The Geraldine Fibbers**
**What Part Of Get Thee Gone Don't You Understand?**

Sympathy For The Record Industry, 1996

*A reissue of* Get Thee Gone *with extra live tracks. Beck represented by his contributions to 'Blue Cross' as before. Great album title, by the way.*

## Various Artists
## Suburbia Soundtrack

DGC, 1997

*From the Richard Linklater movie, with a score by Sonic Youth. Beck's track is a new version of 'Feather In Your Cap' from 1994.*

## Various Artists
## KXLU Demolisten Vol. 2

No Life, 1996

*Radio session compilation on which Beck is definitely the most famous artist. He contributes a version of 'Untitled'.*

## Various Artists
## Kill The Moonlight Soundtrack

Sympathy For The Record Industry, 1997

*The film that inspired 'Loser' was always going to feature Beck on its soundtrack, an album which seems to be the same length as the actual movie. Beck contributes 'Leave Me On The Moon' and 'Underwater Music'.*

## Various Artists
## Modern Day Paintings By Original Music Artists

Fingerpaint, 1997

*Fingerpaint released* A Western Harvest Field by Moonlight *and from it comes 'Lampshade'.*

## Various Artists
## A Life Less Ordinary Soundtrack

A&M, 1997

*A lifeless, ordinary film by all accounts, the best thing about this movie is its soundtrack, and the best thing about its soundtrack is Beck, who gives the world of cinema the specially-composed Latino splendor of 'Deadweight'.*

## Carl Stephenson
## Forest For The Trees

Dreamworks, 1997

*From the Geto Boys to this has been a long journey for Carl Stephenson, who recorded this album in 1994, but elected not to release it then. Beck sings backing vocals on 'Infinite Cow' and plays harmonica on 'Fall'.*

## Various Artists
## WBCN Naked Disc

Wicked Disc, 1997

*A compilation of specially-recorded live tracks from Boston's WBCN. Beck contributes a recently-recorded version of 'One Foot In The Grave'.*

## Various Artists
## Horde Festival 1997

Hollywood 1997

*This promotional CD was put out by the Horde Festival's promoters. Beck is represented by 'Jack-Ass'.*

## Various Artists
## Tibetan Freedom Concert

Grand Royal/Capitol, 1997

*This triple CD benefit record, which came out on the Beastie Boys' own label, is an epic collection of live performances from San Francisco and New York (there is also an interactive CD-ROM). Beck contributes one of his best songs, 'Asshole'.*

## Various Artists
## Bridge School Concert Vol. 1

Reprise, 1997

*The Bridge School is an educational organization closely associated with Neil Young. This compilation of ten years of live shows benefits the Bridge School. Beck performs 'It's All In Your Mind' and, in the company of Don Henley, Patti Smith and Simon and Garfunkel, may be the youngest person here.*

## Select Magazine Beck Promo

Select Magazine, 1996

*Select is an excellent British music magazine and they are the only people in the world ever to devote an entire CD to three tracks by Beck. Those three (particularly well-chosen) tracks are 'Clock', 'The Little Drum Machine Boy' and 'Totally Confused'.*

## Various Artists
## Hear You Me!

Vast, 1998

*Beck contributes 'Silently'. 'Hear You Me!' is a tribute to Weezer fans Mykel and Carli, who were killed in a car crash the year before.*

## Air
## Sexy Boy

Caroline, 1998

*Air, or Air French Band as they are sometimes rather splendidly called, were one of the best new French acts of the 1990s, with a sound somewhere between dance music and James Bond soundtracks. Their debut single, 'Sexy Boy', is available in several mixes, but none more inventive than Beck's 'Sex Kino' mix.*

## Various Artists
## Selector Dub Narcotic

K, 1998

*A compilation of K Acts, naturally featuring Beck and Calvin Johnson, on 'Close To God'.*

## Bjork
## Hunter

Elektra France, 1998

*He's remix crazy! Once again, Beck mixes for France, this time for a French-only B-side version of Homogenic's 'Alarm Call' – under the utterly apt name of Bjeck.*

## Amnesia
## Lingus

Supreme/Island, 1998

*Brad Laner, once of Medicine, enlists Beck, the alt.Stevie Wonder, to play harmonica on 'Drop Down'. Beck's dad David Campbell does the strings on 'Swimming Lessons', 'Train Try' and 'Leaving'.*

## Various Artists
## CMJ New Music Monthly

CMJn, 1998

*This time with Beck on the cover of the mag, and 'Cold Brains' on the CD.*

## Kahimi Karie
## Kahimi Karie

Minty Fresh, 1998

*Karie goes out with maverick Japanese artiste Cornelius. Beck plays harmonica on the revoltingly-named 'Lolitapop Dollhouse'.*

## Various Artists
## The Rugrats Movie Soundtrack

Interscope Records, 1998

*While Satan often crops up in Beck's music, it seemed unlikely until now that he was recommending career choices to him. But here he is on the movie soundtrack to the show that is a* Peanuts *for the 21st century, only more cloying, singing on 'This World Is Something New To Me', which also features Laurie Anderson, the B52s, Lenny Kravitz, Iggy Pop and Lou Rawls. This is what happens when ex-members of Devo (Mark Mothersbaugh) go bad.*

**Bjork**
**Alarm Call**

---

Elektra, 1998

*'Alarm Call' now comes out as an actual single elsewhere in the world and look, it's the Bjeck remix again.*

**Various Artists**
**The Hi-Lo Country Soundtrack**

---

TVT Soundtrax, 1999

*Country music rears its lovely head, Beck gets to be on the same album as Hank Williams, and duets on Floyd Tillman's 'Drivin' Nails In My Coffin' with the great Willie Nelson.*

**Various Artists**
**Wired Magazine Presents Music Futurists**

---

Rhino, 1999

*Among the music futurists are Godley & Creme, Sonic Youth and Tangerine Dream. Beck contributes the futuristic 'Total Soul Future (Eat It)'.*

**Various Artists**
**The Best Latin Party In The World... Ever**

Virgin, USA, 1999

*Ah, 'Burro'... there had to be a place for it somewhere.*

**Various Artists**
**More Oar: A Tribute To Alexander 'Skip' Spence**

Birdman, 1999

*A tribute album to Moby Grape's maverick and addled frontman, badly received at the time, despite the presence of Beck's cover of Spence's 'Halo Of Gold'.*

**Various Artists**
**Return Of The Grievous Angel: A Tribute To Gram Parsons**

Almo Sounds, 1999

*A rather plodding tribute to an electric talent, with reverence overwhelming inspiration. Beck, duetting with Emmylou Harris, at least makes a decent fist of 'Sin City'.*

## Various Artists
## MOM III: Music For Our Mother Ocean

Surf Dog Records, 1999

*Eco-cause types like Paul McCartney, the Beastie Boys and, er, Butthole Surfers make summery or oceany music. Beck contributes the aptly named 'Electric Music And The Summer People'.*

## Various Artists
## SNL 25: Saturday Night Live Musical Performance Volume 2

Dreamworks, 1999

*Beck performs a live version of the wonderful 'Nobody's Fault But My Own'.*

## Various Artists
## MTV – The First 100 Years: Rock

Rhino, 1999

*Massive MTV fan Beck appears on predictable compilation and gives them 'Devil's Haircut'.*

## Various Artists
## The Ultimate Grammy Box Set

Sony/Legacy, 1999

*Four CDs of Grammy winners from the dawn of time up. Beck is here, somewhere, with 'Where It's At', as is Frankie Yankovic, polka king and dad of 'Loser'-satirizing Weird Al.*

## Various Artists
## At Home With The Groovebox

Grand Royal Records, 2000

*Grand Royal gave various people Groovebox synthesizers, whatever they are, and let them do their thing. Beck's thing is called 'Boyz'.*

## Various Artists
## Jane Magazine Winter CD No 6

Jane Magazine, 1999/2000

*Subscribe to* Jane Magazine *and get a CD – with 'Sexx Laws' on it.*

# COVER VERSIONS

The following songs by other people are known to have been performed by Beck, live or on record.

Electric Avenue (Eddie Grant)
Pass The Dutchie (Musical Youth)
He's A Mighty Good Leader (Mississippi John Hurt)
Halo Of Gold (Skip Spence)
Don't You Mind People Grinnin' In Your Face? (Son House)
Drivin' Nails In My Coffin (Jerry Irby)
Fourteen Rivers, Fourteen Floods (Mississippi John Hurt)
Sin City (Gram Parsons)
I'm So Green (Can)
I've Seen The Land Beyond (Mississippi John Hurt)
Waiting For A Train (Jimmy Rodgers)

## THREE

# THE LEGACY

Beck Hansen fits the blueprint for a truly original artist in one very striking way: before he came along, no-one was making the kind of music that he made. (You could also add that after he came along, quite a few people were.) Whatever someone's opinion of Beck and his music may be, there's no denying that unlike several other acts – Lenny Kravitz, Stone Temple Pilots, Blink 182 to name but three groups who have not so much jumped on various old bandwagons as leapt up at the bandwagon and chinned themselves on the fender – Beck invented a music all of his own and filled a gap that previously no-one had even noticed existed.

Arguably, Beck filled quite a few gaps. He was not the inventor of anti-folk, but he did create a version of it that acquired a certain popularity. He brought humour and surrealism back into rock, and particularly American rock, at a time when rock took itself so seriously that it was in danger of bursting into tears and hiding in its bedroom forever. And he proved to a generation whose idea of a blues record was Hootie & The Blowfish and whose connection to folk was Jewel that there was a link between Woody Guthrie and Mississippi John Hurt and a line of raw, acoustic music that predated the flatulent musical self-abuse sessions of *MTV Unplugged* by about fifty years.

Most of all, though, Beck made the brilliantly simple link between hip hop and folk in one move, in one record in fact. By recording 'Loser', Beck not only ended the need for pop academics to blather on obviously about how hip hop was a new urban folk, but by demonstrating the fact via the medium of a four-minute song, he nailed the two genres together for ever with the solid, basic gesture of rapping a folk song over hip hop beats. The addition of Doctor John's swamp rock 'Walk On Gilded Splinters' riff and slide guitar just served to nail everything together even more solidly. 'Loser' is one of those classic records – like The Sex Pistols' 'Anarchy In The UK', like James Brown's 'Sex Machine', like Kraftwerk's 'Autobahn' – that invents a genre instantly, on one side of a small piece of plastic.

If Beck had retired after recording 'Loser', he would a) have been completely insane and b) still have invented a new kind of music single-handedly and irreversibly. This would have been enough of an achievement to place him in the fat, dusty annals of rock forever (although to do so in reality means recording hundreds and hundreds of albums of increasingly poor quality and thereby achieving 'classic' status). Fortunately, Beck didn't retire, but went on (and goes on) to record more and more inventive music. (And, of course, 'Loser' isn't Beck's first record; he had been recording cassettes and had released 'MTV Makes Me Want To Smoke Crack' already – this was an overnight star with a history).

A brief look at Beck's recorded career – which barely spans a half-decade – indicates that he has a versatility and restlessness which would shame a hundred other supposed eclectic artistes who get along on two or three mild changes of direction which no-one has ever noticed. (Bon Jovi, for example, for whom a haircut is a change of direction. For them, the onset of male pattern baldness would be the equivalent of an *Unplugged* album.) Beck's has made a virtue out of diversity, experiment and the need to try something different on each record.

There's the acoustic, banjo-accompanied, acerbic novelty music of *Golden Feelings*, which ought to sound like anyone could have made it but clearly evokes the opposite reaction. There's the wild raving of *Stereopathetic Soul Manure*, which sounds like a B-side collection from an alternative universe and ranges from silly tape experiments to railroad songs sung by a hobo, from daft tunes about Ozzy Osbourne to beautiful country pastiches, from feedback punk to strange blues. There's the cold and autumnal *One Foot In The Grave*, which represents Beck as a folk-blues singer, but still manages to throw in some strange, almost avant-garde curveballs, and as an album would, for most acts, have been a launching pad for a style, not a one-off. There's the acoustic oddness of *A Western Harvest Field By Moonlight*, and – in the same year – there's *Mellow Gold*, the record that took Beck's mixture of folk and hip hop into the mainstream, and proved that songs like 'Nitemare Hippy Girl' and 'Whiskeyclone' could be the stuff of hit albums (and this was also Beck's fourth album release of the year. Even David Bowie never changed styles midstream that often.)

There's *Odelay*, Beck's second collaboration (if you count *One Foot In The Grave*) and a very different one, on which The Dust Brothers create a sympathetic environment for Beck's expanding musical range and manage to take elements of 1960s rock, blues and folk and make them sound utterly contemporary. There's *Mutations*, which has the spooky, dreamy feel of Radiohead's *OK Computer* (both produced by Nigel Godrich) with elements of Beck blues and folk and a strange atmosphere that's simultaneously reminiscent of The Beatles' *White Album* and also sounds totally modern. And there's *Midnite Vultures*, which Beck regards as the official follow-up to *Odelay*, but which sounds more like the follow-up to Prince's *Sign Of The Times*. And none of this takes into account the enormous flow of B-sides and contributions to other people's projects as song-writer and even remixer which Beck has managed to generate, and whose variety and regularity would have floored a lesser artist. Beck is so prolific, you begin to suspect that he's not a musician at all, he's a virus.

This does not mean that Beck is no good, chucking records out like an incontinent hound. There's a very strong case to be made for the idea that prolificness is a sign of musical talent. Not all of the following are a direct influence on Beck, but in their various heydays, Prince, Bowie, Dylan, The Beatles, Neil Young, The Rolling Stones and – a comparable talent who will be mentioned again here – Elvis Costello were all distinguished as artists, not only by the quality of their work but the quantity of it. The Beatles and The Stones managed to turn out two and sometimes three albums a year, with accompanying singles and unique B-sides, and absolutely no indication that this affected the quality of their work (quite the opposite in fact, as though the 1960s were a musical hothouse). Bowie and Dylan not only seemed to knock off an album a day, but to give themselves a complete stylistic makeover every time they did so (Bowie fans are still reeling from the shock they felt after the release of *Never Let Me Down* in the 1980s – not that it was bad, although it was, but that Bowie had the same image as last time.) At his best, Prince was unable to confine himself in any way, producing for others, making so many records he had to release triple albums (and even making a spare album, *The Black Album*), and generally being so prolific that his record company claimed they could not promote his excess of product. And all of the above examples of musical prolificness and diversity apply to Neil Young, who as time goes by for both of them, seems increasingly to be Beck's nearest artistic contemporary, with his seeming folksiness disguising a powerful imagination that won't be limited by mere rock music (even if Young hasn't gone hip hop, he did do an electro-rock album).

Elvis Costello is also close to the Beck model. Beginning as a folk act, Costello's music was radically altered by two other musical genres – the traditionalist, back-to-roots pub rock and the out-of-nowhere controversy of punk, as Beck was with blues and hip hop. Similarly, within minutes of establishing himself as a new kind of singer (in his case, violently paranoid and aggressive but also capable of tenderness and melody), Costello changed his sound for his second album, and did it again on his third album, and his fourth album, and his fifth album and so on. Like Beck, Costello's records are often reactions to his previous records; thus an amphetamine-fuelled punk album will be followed by an acoustic country rock album, a Euro-pop tribute by a 1960s soul collection, a collaboration with a string quartet by a splenetic rocker. Like Beck he favours humour and emotional honesty in his lyrics, but can write songs whose words are almost impenetrable. Like Beck, he is clearly extremely intelligent, often standing back from the events, emotions and people he is writing about. And like Beck he is astonishingly prolific.

Interestingly, and probably because of all the above factors, many of these artists have also shown a fondness for pseudonyms. Costello as The Imposter, Prince as The Artist, Bowie as Ziggy Stardust, and even Neil Young once pretended to be a rockabilly act. This book sticks its neck out and says, watch out for Beck appearing under some false names near you soon...

Beck's position in music is a unique one. He is a successful musician in the commercial arena or, as we prefer to say, a pop star. Like most pop stars, he is attractive, entertaining and can dance. Like most pop stars, his records sell around the world, young girls like him, and young boys hate it that young girls like him (there are lots of Beck websites run by boys out there which contain disclaimers like 'all you stupid girls, this is a SERIOUS site'). He tours, he has hits, he makes videos, he's part of pop culture in the way that previous would-be musical mixers like Britain's often excellent Pop Will Eat Itself or the plodding Living Colour never were.

However, unlike most pop stars, Beck has an extraordinarily rootsy background for a modern artist. Beck began his career playing the acoustic guitar in his bedroom, listening to old records, and performing on street corners and small clubs. He knows the art of crowd-pleasing – he regrets much of his early output, regarding it as novelty music to keep audiences from falling asleep – but he's also a genuine musician. He may not play long guitar solos or compose miniature three-act rock operas, but Beck's records – no matter how commercial or fun or even funny – are rooted in musicianship. He may sing about two turntables and a microphone, but Beck's life as a musician began with six strings and a bedroom.

This is obviously not that completely unusual in popular music, unless you are one of N'Sync (and even they presumably like to hunker down with the jumbo acoustic every now and then); Beck's ability to play and his learning the guitar in his bedroom are staples of the rock star success story. Everyone from John Lennon to Joe Perry started like that, playing along to their favourite records or learning the guitar from books written by men who looked like old gardeners on parole. (Those who did not pretended they could, and played tennis rackets in front of a mirror; they are now singers.) The difference between Beck and almost all the other rock musicians is, again, the roots aspect. Musically speaking, most musicians do not go back further than about one generation when they start learning to play. Bands of the 1990s listened to 1980s records, 1970s rockers were influenced by 1960s groups, 1960s musicians had the 1950s to fall back on, and so on and so forth. This often has a weakening effect on music, as musical styles become diluted rather than thicker and stronger; knowledge of previous musics is diffused and thus a teenager hearing, say, Willie Dixon's 1950s song 'You Need Love' will think that for some reason an old black man has decided to record Led Zeppelin's 1970s tune 'Whole Lotta Love'.

But what makes Beck different is that he didn't just listen to a Suzanne Vega album or a couple of Sheryl Crow songs and say, wow, I'm a folkie now; he went right back to the roots of modern music, meaning here the roots of all modern music, from pop and dance to rock and rap. At a time when everyone else in LA was practising their Van Halen riffs, Beck was listening to the blues, to folk music, to Mississippi John Hurt and Woody Guthrie. Where most 'roots-based' American rock is copied from Aerosmith's version of The Rolling Stones' version of the blues or Led Zeppelin's version of Bert Jansch's version of folk, Beck ignored the bad photocopies and went back to the original blueprint. He is one of the few musicians working in the twenty-first century who felt the need to start at base.

And his choice of favourite roots music is interesting, too. When Beck bought a Gibson acoustic because his hero Woody Guthrie had one, he wasn't just tapping into any old folk tradition. Beck, who has specifically disdained and mocked the hippy 'folk' tradition of songs about lovely flowers and pretty streams, chose to adopt the hardest, rawest version of folk, a proletarian blues about struggle and tears. Woody Guthrie was a hero to him because Guthrie tried to sing about the truth, not about getting together in a nice valley. (If Beck had been English, the folk tradition he would have had to draw on was even more scary, based as it is on people singing about fair maids round the may pole, tra la, in a terrifying 1920s version of the rural idyll. No wonder the most interesting folk-influenced musician in the UK, Billy Bragg, came to folk via punk rock and socialism.)

More extremely, Beck's take on blues is a particularly interesting one. Most rock music is derived from the electric blues of Chicago and the Northern states, where the amplified guitar went from being a necessity to the exciting backbone of a new music. Beck didn't like the electric blues. He preferred the 'delta' blues, the rural, acoustic kind, generally played by old men still wearing their field overalls. Often these old men were retired gents who had been persuaded to put their field overalls on by young students, who felt that the blues was more authentic sung by a man who looked like he had just got in from a hard day's farm work. But Beck clearly liked the odour of authenticity, the idea that this was the real thing.

More seriously, there is unarguably also a stronger element of spirituality in the delta blues, something which seems to appeal to Beck with his various lyrical references to Satan and death.

Beck once said of blues singer Skip James, 'When he sings about the Devil, you get a feeling of evil.' (Oddly, Beck has no time for the most revered blues singer, the 'king of delta blues', Robert Johnson.)

Beck's influences go way back in time to the dawn of popular music as we know it; thus, when Beck sings, he does so in an old man's voice, and he does so because his knowledge of, and love for, music started with records made by singers who were dead before many of Beck's audience were born. It's true that Beck is not alone in this. There are student bars and folk clubs and coffee houses all around the world full of young people with one finger in their ear and the other in the cottonfields, singing blues and folk and updating it in their own way for a modern audience. Acoustic music is not dead, and artists as diverse as Tracy Chapman and Steve Earle have written hundreds of superb songs that have taken an old tradition forward into modern times. The blues lives on, too, in the music of lots of awful people, from the besuited bore Eric Clapton to the equally snooze-inducing Robert Cray, and, a little more excitingly, in boogie bands like Aerosmith and in the better moments of old codgers like Page and Plant.

Beck is not the first person to have heard some old records. Where he does differ is in the way he's interpreted those records. Most people who have heard old records seem to have been paralysed by them and to have stood still musically ever since (with the occasional exception of ZZ Top, who are secretly an art concept band like Roxy Music disguised as three old rockers with beards). Like the trad jazz bands of the 1960s, who were recreating a music that was dead in 1930 because they hated what it had become, blues bands and folk singers cling on to the past because they hate the present (imagine if the only group in the world was one of those bar band Blues Brothers clones. Then shudder.)

And the problem that blues and folk create for musicians is that, because these kinds of music are valued for their authenticity, musicians feel that by tampering with them, they will remove the authenticity and somehow become big old fakes. (It doesn't seem to occur to these musicians that anybody playing the blues who is not actually a seventy-five-year-old black man who grew up on a farm in the Deep South is something of a big old fake anyway. Likewise, most British folk singers tend to conveniently forget that they are not Blondel the mandolin player sitting outside Richard I's cell in 1194.)

What Beck did, and may have been the first person to do, was realize on an intuitive (as opposed to a write-an-essay) kind of level that blues and folk are, by and large, the same as rap and hip hop. The differences between them – time, big drums, gold chains – are, musically, irrelevant. All these kinds of music were street music, music made in the most basic and immediate way. More importantly, they had direct, powerful lyrics that were sometimes funny, frequently topical and almost always emotional. While it would be the mark of an idiot to say that, if Woody Guthrie was around today, he would be working with Doctor Dre, it's not silly to say that Woody Guthrie has a lot more in common with Chuck D and Rage Against The Machine than he does with some fool busker on the subway warbling his or her way through 'Where Have All The Flowers Gone?' Beck saw a direct connection between these musics and, instead of conceptualizing about it, went into Carl Stephenson's house and recorded 'Loser'. Maybe there was an element of luck here, but the fact that the two men hit it off, that Stephenson related to the slide guitar riff Beck played and Beck related to the hip hop loops that Stephenson played, indicates that Beck was right and had a musical vision which was about to come true.

Beck saw the real authenticity of folk and blues and in doing so, overturned the tedium of years of stereotyping. There is a long history of struggle between authenticity and fun. On the political left, authenticity was king and all protest songs were written on acoustic guitars so as not to be corrupted by capitalism. It was felt that elements like amplifiers, overdubs, multi-tracking and the like were somehow dishonest, and detracted from the truth of the songs (even now, Billy Bragg, a man who has diverse tastes and has not been afraid to be involved in dance music, takes up the simple wooden guitar to sing Woody Guthrie's lyrics).

The result of this philosophy was not, oddly, to convert the world to left-wing politics and folk clubs, but to drive most people – who now felt they were being regarded as scum just because they liked a tune – away as far as possible from simple honest acoustic music. Folk clubs became seen as ludicrous places where people with comedy beards got together to sing in comedy voices to other people with comedy beards. Folk singers were seen as posturing ponces in black sweaters who smoked too many French cigarettes. Worst of all, instead of being relevant to real life, folk music became as distant from real life as Etruscan pottery. (Even the most important folk-influenced pop star of the twentieth century, Bob Dylan, realized this as early as 1965 when he moved with admirable speed from being an acoustic troubadour to a full-on folk rocker with guitar, bass, drums and organ. It was a major defeat for authenticity, but a great day for fun.)

When folk (and to a similar extent, blues) did return in the late 1960s and early 1970s, as part of America's new quest for simplicity and honesty and the British hippy craze for 'getting it together in the country', it was as a testicle-less beast, a vague, drooling nincompoop of a music that smoked dope, wore beads and mouthed platitudes. Guthrie and Dylan had been specific about the nature of social problems; the new folkies just burbled about how it would be nice if we all got on, as though the Vietnam war was a mild dispute at a family wedding between Uncle Jim and cousin Edie. Worst of all, the Laurel Canyon post-folkies like James Taylor and Linda Ronstadt were only interested in describing their tiresome love lives in voices that would have sent a crystal meth addict to sleep. Folk faded out again in the 1970s, lullabied to death.

In this context, what Beck did was quite remarkable, something that no-one had managed to do for twenty years; he made folk and blues not only acceptable, but also exciting. When 'Loser' came out, it was such a confident record that, even though it had quite silly lyrics, no-one dismissed it as a novelty single. People noticed that Beck had found a way to combine the latest music – hip hop – with two of the oldest – folk and blues – and they liked it. 'Loser' helped to redefine popular music, and the albums that followed took music into new and increasingly interesting areas.

Beck did not arise in isolation. His music sounds very little like grunge – although some of his punkier tracks, particularly the louder moments on *Stereopathetic Soul Manure*, could be Nirvana demos – but it dovetails neatly with that sound. America likes its acoustic rockers to be clean and polite, and Beck – although doubtless hygienic and never rude – was never going to be those things. He needed a climate to nurture him and to allow him his place in the sun. And 'Loser' fitted the sound of the times. Not that blues and folk were all the rage (although, as has been mentioned, Nirvana had even recorded Leadbelly's old blues 'Where Did You Sleep Last Night?', giving it a fantastic undertow of menace), but rather that, as something of a reaction to the colourful but stupid poodle metal of the past few years, grunge had become popular. Often lumped in, like Beck, with slackers and other middle-class idle idiots, grunge was one of the most exciting forms of American rock.

Bands like Nirvana and Pearl Jam made honesty and directness an issue, invented a new form of rock that hadn't been heard before, Nirvana playing a roaring slow/fast blast of emotional punk, Pearl Jam an extraordinary low, rusty train sound best described by one critic (i.e., me) as 'chumbling', and – more importantly for the style papers – went round dressed in cheap plaid shirts and bad jeans. Grunge made emotion and honesty important again in American music (in Britain, music hall was undergoing one of its periodic revivals) and this, combined with its mixture of lethargic vocals and animated playing, helped to create a climate where someone like Beck – who just did not sound like Mötley Crüe – could make an impact, both musically and in the charts.

Equally importantly, hip hop was coming to dominate the white pop arena. While it has never needed a white audience to make it any good, hip hop had, with a few exceptions, not yet become the favourite music of white America. It was popular with white critics and college kids but not, by and large, completely accepted in the pop arena (bands like Public Enemy and Run DMC, while massive, were always perceived as somehow more classier and 'relevant' than others).

But now, with the rise of West Coast rap, hip hop was part of white America's pop blood. It was time for someone to really make a crossover record. There had been crossovers before, but not immensely successful, lasting ones. Vanilla Ice had sold a lot of records but only succeeded in hammering home a public perception of himself as a white-haired dolt. Run DMC and Aerosmith's 'Walk This Way' had famously only revived one band's career – Aerosmith's – while The Beastie Boys, who'd enjoyed enormous success with the jock-punk-rap of *Licensed To Ill*, had seen their fame run away laughing from them when they attempted something more serious with their follow-up album, *Paul's Boutique* (produced by The Dust Brothers – who significantly had a lot more luck when they came to work with Beck on *Odelay*).

There was a space for a white hip hop record, and there was a space for a grunge record that people could actually dance around and have fun to (great though they were, Nirvana were rarely a fun band. Even when thrashing about like armless apes on the awesome 'Smells Like Teen Spirit', they seemed to be annoyed about something as usual, and would later complain about the record's production). 'Loser' filled that gap, and, best of all, it was funny without being inane. Young people could sing along to it, jerk about spasmodically, and most excitingly, feel cool while at the same time looking down on people who felt cool.

It's also worth remembering what else was around at the time of Beck's irresistible rise. In 1994 the American charts were amenable to grunge and hip hop but essentially they were the kind of place that the American charts have always been. In summer of that year, big American hits did include 'Fantastic Voyage' by Coolio and Warren G and Nate Dogg's superb 'Regulate' – a verb, by the way, that seems to be one of Beck's favourites, as he has used it in nearly every interview he's ever done – but the charts were also enlivened by Elton John's 'Can You Feel The Love Tonight?', Mariah Carey's 'Anytime You Need A Friend' and Big Mountain's Framptastic cover version of 'Baby I Love Your Way'. R&B was represented by R. Kelly's subtle 'Your Body's Callin' ' (great title for a Beck song, by the way) and Boyz II Men's ambiguous 'I'll Make Love To You'. But with the possible exception of Crash Test Dummies and Lisa Loeb, there was little around that could be described as either 'alternative' (Beck's least favourite word) or as outside the most mainstream of mainstream. Musically, America seemed to have unscrewed its head and put it in a closet for a moment. In this context, 'Loser' sounded like a breath of loud air.

The situation was not dissimilar in the UK, a country where the 1980s seemed to be so strongly revived that Prince, Madonna and Bruce Springsteen were all enjoying enormous success ('The Most Beautiful Girl In The World', 'I'll Remember', and 'Streets Of Philadelphia' respectively), while Bon Jovi and, weirdly, Guns 'n' Roses were charting. Buzzing around these torpid diplodocuses were the usual pop acts – Let Loose, Eternal, East 17 – who mean nothing in the USA, and the twin kings of Britpop, Oasis and Blur. There it was a better time, at least for pop music, but innovation outside dance music was virtually dead.

The 1990s were at least a time of variety, but the decade that Beck came of musical age in, the 1980s, was appalling. There is a tired old phrase about the 1970s being the decade that taste forgot, but at least it was a musically astonishing decade, a huge spectrum of talent from Chic and Funkadelic, to Bowie and Kraftwerk, Led Zeppelin and The Who, to The Clash and The Sex Pistols, Bob Marley and Lee Perry, to Stevie Wonder and Marvin Gaye, and a million others who refined their earlier work or invented something new. The 1980s were not such a decade. After a promising start with post-punk acts, 1980s pop and rock was a bland affair that substituted experiment for hair and pants for talent. The only real innovation of the era that lasted was rap. The 1980s wasn't entirely made up of A Flock Of Seagulls and The Fixx, it just felt like it. During this decade, American music was at its most artificial, and as a musician Beck only had two choices: he could either go along with this, or he could react against it. Fortunately for popular music, he chose to react against it.

It would be interesting to see how Beck's musicianly career would have panned out if he had not been born in America. While it would be the act of a fat fool to say that American music at the time was inferior to British, European, African or Asian music, the fact remains that, at the end of the 1980s, when not a lot was going on in American pop, on the other side of the ocean, the most exciting musical shift in British music, acid house, was taking place. The acid house boom tore apart the foundations of British pop and youth culture and spread into everyone's lives, from rock fans to the Houses of Parliament. Barely talented rock groups like The Stone Roses (goth) and The Soup Dragons (1960s revivalists) were galvanized into making good records, while bands with real talent – The Happy Mondays prime amongst them – produced some of the best music of the decade. It would have been fascinating to hear Beck's reaction to this music. As it is, while acid house has ramifications in the world's music even now over a decade later, it never had very much effect on American music. Britain and Europe suffered a seismic shift of musical sensibilities in the 1980s; America didn't. In many ways, at the beginning of the 1990s, it was still a land fit for Pat Benatar.

Growing up in this era, it's easy to see how Beck turned out the way he did. About half of his music is a reaction against what was going on when he was a kid – from the ironic title of the feedback-crazed 'Pink Noise (Rock Me Amadeus)' and the shouted lyric of 'Ozzy', he was not part of the 1980s scene. The honesty and sparseness of anti-folk was as much a protest against Duran Duran and Van Halen as it was against the New York folk scene. Singing songs by Mississippi John Hurt and Skip James was the polar opposite of covering Bruce Springsteen songs in a bar. The other half of Beck's music – the dance half – is a tribute to Beck's musical past, from the hip-hop beats of 'Loser' to the R&B grooves of 'Sexx Laws'. He has always loved the funk, and this sets him apart from almost any other alternative act, nearly all of whom have their roots in white rock music of some kind.

In fact, one of the most exciting areas of Beck's music which can't really be documented here is his live work. While on record, Beck can be dry and droll, and his music appear deliberately lethargic and slow-paced, onstage Beck is a dance monster, who one minute can be executing James Brown-style dance moves and the next is preaching like a boggle-eyed minister to the crowd. As someone who has absorbed the stagecraft of black music and its life (you don't come out of a Metallica show feeling that you have danced your ass off), Beck stands out from almost every other 'alternative' artist ever.

And of course on *Midnite Vultures* he stands out from almost every other funk and dance artist ever. With the huge exceptions of George Clinton and Sly Stone and, to a lesser extent, Prince, Beck is one of the few artists ever to add psychedelic-style surrealism and Dylanesque lyric writing to funk. He famously once met up with the R&B act Boyz II Men to work on a track but it all went wrong when Beck began making up absurd words to the song they were trying to record, and Boyz II Men disappeared, never to return. In some areas, it seems, convention cannot be overturned. Which is a pity; the lyrical insights of 'Hollywood Freaks' and 'Mixed Bizness' would do a lot for the otherwise romance-based shagadelic lyrics of most modern soul music (then again, maybe Beck just got on Boyz II Men's tits).

As a lyricist, Beck is unique. From the famous 'I'm a loser, baby/so why don't you kill me?' couplet of 'Loser', to 'Brief encounters in Mercedes Benz/Wearing hepatitis contact lens/Bed and breakfast getaway weekends/With Sports Illustrated moms', in 'Sexx Laws' his writing is an extraordinary mixture of styles. His main obsession is decay. His songs constantly refer to death, rotting, emptiness and trash (Beck is the most litter-obsessed writer of his era), and he delivers them in a languid, deadpan fashion that utterly suits lines like 'Night birds will cackle/Rotting like apples on trees/Sending their dead melodies to me' ('Dead Melodies') or 'Temperature's dropping at the rotting oasis/Stealing kisses from the leprous faces' ('Devil's Haircut'). Even on the funky, apparently sex-obsessed groove lyrics of *Midnite Vultures*, the emphasis is on the rot at the heart of LA culture (you can't be a vulture until you have something dead to eat).

Fortunately, for us and for Beck's record label, Beck's lyrical obsessions are tempered with humour. His hatred of novelty songs has not stopped him being a funny songwriter. From 'Truck-Drivin Neighbors' and 'Karaoke weekend at the suicide shack/Community service and I'm still the mack', Beck has always been a great observational songwriter, able to pin down characters and situation with powerful wit.

Beck is a songwriter who loves words. Admittedly, often for their own sake – he's written his fair share of doggerel – but his nonsense is generally a lot better than other people's nonsense. It's interesting that, for someone who went through anti-folk's rigorous disciplines, and for someone who's such a fan of the stark, often monosyllabic writing of Hurt and Guthrie, that the lyricist Beck often most resembles – in his choice of words, that is, rather than themes – is the Bob Dylan of *Blonde On Blonde*, who blinded America with glittering imagery. A line like 'with your diamonds, your amphetamines and your fog' is a clear precursor of the Beck lyrical style, while this quote from Beck, where he is discussing songwriting – 'Set your guitars and banjos on fire, and before you write a song, smoke a pack of whiskey and it'll all take care of itself' – could easily have come from one of Dylan's legendary 1960s press conferences.

There are two traditional lyrical strands in American music, which come from American literature and certain differing attitudes to life. The first is the straightforward, plain-talking tradition which is connected to the American view of America as a rough-hewn country, knocked into shape by pioneers, cowboys and pilgrims. This tradition gives us not only the sturdy prose of Stephen King and the films of John Wayne and Clint Eastwood, but also the music of Woody Guthrie and the most recent work of Bruce Springsteen. Bruce Springsteen is also a bridge into the other tradition of American music. His early work was characterized, not by plain-speaking songs about factories and family delivered by a man in jeans, but by flowery, almost incomprehensible lyrics about jesters and kings and street ladies and God knows what else sung by a heavily-bearded Bruce while wearing a knitted hat. This was at a time when Springsteen was hugely influenced by Bob Dylan, who, with his jokers and kings and queens, seems to have used a pack of cards as lyrical inspiration for much of his work.

This other tradition is the romantic, wordy side of American music, brought into pop by Bob Dylan, who was very good at it, and who got it off the beat poets, people like Jack Kerouac and Allen Ginsberg, who were often very good at it too, but equally often made you want to knock them to the ground. Beat poetry favoured emotion at full pitch over emotions recalled in tranquillity, spontaneity over rewrites and considered thought, and, at its best, managed to graft a huge romantic vision of life, all leaping up and down like a French poet addled by absinthe, onto a version of modern America. Jazz and black leather were part of the deal, and the whole thing was all doped-up and youthful and a great reaction against Eisenhower's mom-and-apple-pie America.

Beck is unusual because his records seem to go towards one of these traditions, run back to the other and then swing back. Just as his albums go from folky lo-fi sincerity to big budget panoramic dance, so he seems reluctant to engage one form or the other. As a lyricist, he can often be obscure and poetically wordy; but his heroes wrote plain, simple and effective songs that he admires for their honesty and directness. As a performer, he likes to dress up and put on a show and generally be something of a wild man on stage; but as a pop star, he is full of doubt about his work, comes across as a normal (if witty) human being in interviews and hardly seems to wallow in luxury like his contemporaries. It's as if he sees the irony in what he does too clearly, and steps back at the last minute (you could never imagine Beck, say, changing his name to The Artist Formerly Known As Beck or buying a gold-plated limousine; it would strike him as silly. That said, he'll probably do it now.)

This is the central point about Beck. He won't be tied to anything. For a pop star, or a musician, or an artiste, he is extraordinarily reticent about committing himself to many of the follies that pop stars and musicians and artistes commit to on a daily basis.

Lyrically, Beck is a reticent writer. He either writes character songs ('Truckdrivin' Neighbors'), wild abstractions which refer to himself but obscurely ('Devil's Haircut'), songs about himself which are partly ironic ('Sexx Laws') or songs full of spooky allusions to death and decay (nearly all of *Mutations*). He doesn't favour the personal, confessional song at all; when Beck is writing in the first person, he's normally claiming that the Devil gave him a taco or something equally implausible. Possibly this is a reaction against the singer-songwriter poor-me ethic, but most likely Beck just doesn't feel comfortable with pouring it all out. Just as he sings in an even, almost emotionless voice and refuses to grin and leap about for photos, so he keeps the feeling in his songs on a dead calm even keel.

'I write really personal songs but I would hesitate to put them on record, I have a tendency to keep them for myself,' he said once. 'I'm like a teenager, I like to try on different outfits.' In this he resembles many of the songwriters mentioned before – Bowie in all his different roles, Costello as country singer and soul man, Neil Young as rockabilly or folkie or hard rocker, Prince as various kinds of sex. Interestingly, though, while Beck enjoys a degree of distance, he is not emotion-free. He's not a cynical artist, just a guarded one.

'Cynicism is the easiest attitude a kid can adopt to face the world. But at the same time it can be destructive in the long run, it can stifle your emotions. So I'm walking on a tightrope between cynicism and sincerity', he said once. 'But what I love best in my songs is telling strange stories.'

The strangest story Beck could tell is of course his own. From a bohemian background of no money and a past which needs no added romanticism, he invented himself and forged a completely independent path (at an age when most people are wondering what colour shoes they like best, Beck had already decided what kind of music he was going to play for the rest of his life). Seemingly destined to be one of those semi-busking live performers who's a wow in the local club and ends up a local legend who never left town, Beck created a new music that he took round the world. Having done that, he then invented another one. And having finally shown the world with the success of *Odelay* and *Mutations* that there were two sides to Beck, he released *Midnite Vultures* to show people that there was a third.

Beck is not a man who likes being categorized. Partly this is because the moment he had a hit – 'Loser' – the world wrote 'Slacker' on a box and dropped him in it. Mostly, though, Beck likes to be his own man, and as such is a more varied artist than most will ever be. He takes his music very seriously but sometimes takes the sting out of his own importance by wearing a *Star Wars* stormtrooper mask on stage or writing a song about his friend throwing up. He wants to be a delta blues singer, and he also wants to be R. Kelly. He was involved with anti-folk, a movement thrown up in protest at the tweeness of the post-Dylan singers, and yet Beck, more than anyone else, is a post-Dylan singer.

And, with *Midnite Vultures*, an album that for the first time critics and fans did not instantly 'get', Beck has done it again. He is reluctant to commit to being the man who does *Odelay*-type music over and over. Where before he liked to keep all the strange elements and the dance elements separate from album to album, this time round Beck synthesized them. What he does next is of course a complete mystery, but the only thing that is certain is that it will be unpredictable.

Beck has often talked about what it would be like to be making his thirtieth or fortieth album. The way things are going, he has every chance of finding out.

# INDEX

## PICTURE CREDITS

Picture section page 1: Phil Poynter. 2 top: Liaison; bottom: Pictorial Press. 3 top: Showtime/Pictorial Press; bottom: Liaison. 4 top: Robert Lewis/Pictorial Press; bottom: Rob Verhorst/Pictorial Press. 5 top: Paul Bergen/Redferns; bottom: Ebet Roberts/Redferns. 6 top: Martin Norris/Pictorial Press; bottom Pictorial Press. 7 top: Jon Super/Redferns; bottom Mick Hutson/Redferns. 8: Liaison.